Agee and Actuality:

Artistic Vision in His Work

Agee and Actuality:

Artistic Vision in His Work

by

Victor A. Kramer

The Whitston Publishing Company
Troy, New York
1991

047448 834

Acknowledgements

I want to thank the following journals for publishing my essays and for allowing me to reprint them as revised here:

"The Manuscript and Text of James Agee's *A Death in the Family*," *The Papers of the Bibliographical Society of America*, 65 (Third Quarter 1971), 257-266.

"Agee's Plans for the Criticism of Popular Culture," *Journal of Popular Culture*, 5 (Fall 1972), 755-766.

"Agee's *Let Us Now Praise Famous Men*: Image of Tenant Life," *The Mississippi Quarterly*, 25 (Fall 1972), 405-417.

"Agee's Use of Regional Material in *A Death in the Family*," *Appalachian Journal*, Vol. 1, No. 1 (1972), Appalachian State University, 72-80.

"Agee's Projected Screenplay for Chaplin: Scientists and Tramps," *Southern Humanities Review*, 7 (Fall 1973), 357-364.

"*A Death in the Family* and Agee's Projected Novel," *Proof*, 3 (1973), 139-154.

"'Religion at its deepest intensity' The Stasis of *The Morning Watch*," *Renascence*, 27 (Summer 1975), 221-230.

"Agee's Skepticism about Art and Audience," *The Southern Review*, 17 (Spring 1981), 320-331.

The following two pieces were originally published as chapters in books. Permission has been granted by the University of Alabama Press to reprint the essay about *Let Us Now Praise Famous Men*, "The Consciousness of Technique: The Prose Method of James Agee's *Let Us Now Praise Famous Men*" from *Literature at the Barricades: The American Writer in the 1930s*, edited by Ralph F. Bogardus and Fred Hobson (1982), 114-125.

The essay "James Agee" (originally entitled "A Reconciliation of Forces: James Agee's Life and the Development of His Work as a Writer") first appeared in *Literature of Tennessee*, edited by Ray Willbanks (Macon, Georgia: Mercer University Press, 1984), 133-148.

The paper "Agee's Critical Judgement," the basis for my essay "James Agee's Criticism as Insight into Popular Culture and the Problems of Making an Honest Film," was read at the Florida State University Cinematic Studies Conference: The Freedom to Create, in Tallahassee, Florida, on January 30, 1976.

The paper "Urban and Rural Tension in Agee's Autobiographical *A Death in the Family*" was read at the Southeastern American Studies Association meeting in Atlanta, on April 27, 1972.

I also want to acknowledge my appreciation of the support and encouragement of the James Agee Trust, and its first Trustee, David McDowell, who over the years encouraged me to pursue my various scholarly investigations of Agee. Mr. McDowell's generous approval of my work had made it possible to return to the study of Agee for decades.

Similarly, I want to acknowledge the support and encouragement provided by the University of Texas, its Department of English, and the Humanities Research Center, now called the Harry Ransom Humanities Research Center. Its purchase of the Agee Papers in 1964, and its addition to those papers over the years has facilitated my study. I therefore thank the HRHRC for its consent for me to incorporate within this book Agee materials housed in that library.

Table of Contents

He always wrote. I mean he always, always wrote. Jim never took a day off, basically. If we did something in the evening, then he would come home, sit down, and start writing. I mean he'd never have a full twenty-four hours without doing some writing. Never. If he took a vacation, it was in order to write. It meant being free of having to work for TIME or having to work for whomever. A vacation was time for him to do his own writing.

Mia Fritsch Agee

To art belongs not only the master's skill—the ability to translate a vision into sensual form—but also the ability not to obstruct either the illumining action of the idea or, so to speak, the idea's "generation" and "incarnation" in the mind of the artist. Externally the artist may choose to appear haughty, but interiorly he must be a humbly receptive womb for the "conception." Only if he knows how to be quiet will the *anima* sing in him.

Hans Urs von Balthasar
THE GLORY OF THE LORD:
A Theological Aesthetics. I.
Seeing the Form, p. 251

He couldn't define himself. That was his great trouble as a writer, too. He couldn't limit himself; he was oceanic. And in a way that was his great strength, too.

Dwight Macdonald

Introduction

In all of James Agee's writing, whether an informal sketch or a finished piece of work, he sought to provide his vision of reality, a way of seeing which honors the beauty of what is beheld. Because he wrote in so many different ways, as poet, critic, essayist, fiction writer, experimental writer, it is sometimes possible to overlook the fact that his love of the commonplace world, what he once referred to as "the dignity of actuality," is a concern which consistently informs all his uses of the printed word—from his earliest verbalized dreams of being a writer through the wide variety of all his writings including the manuscript, unfinished at his death, about his own family which became the well known novel *A Death in the Family*.

In the essays which I have written for this book it has not been my concern to analyze Agee's biography or to provide defenses of him as a writer. His varied work speaks for itself. What it says, over and over, is that the world in its particularity is to be honored. The fact is Agee was someone who was fascinated by what could be done with words, but he was also a writer who expressed doubts about the ability of any author to catch the complexity of a world which he insisted must be regarded with respect, awe, and honor. As a writer whose fascination for the world remained so strong throughout his career, and also as one who kept seeking ways to mirror his love and fascination, Agee kept beginning again and again. His accomplished and wide ranging *corpus* documents this.

These studies, ten published as scholarly essays, and two read for meetings, could well be described as my returns to Agee's continuing fascination with the world through words and his various experiments with trying to find adequate ways to mirror his vision of the world. Agee's expression was always one which both had to acknowledge the writer's respect for reality and acknowledge his continuing awareness of the difficulty of what he sought to do. Gathered together these essays provide an overview of Agee's career as a writer, as someone who kept returning to the world he saw with such clarity, a vision he longed to articulate in words. Each of these essays provides an examination of an aspect of Agee's concern for finding ways through words to transmit the beauty of the real world he so loved and which he wanted others to see.

Arranged in seven parts, these essays demonstrate how Agee's work grew out of his observation of the world which he experienced. The opening articles demonstrate how his work grew out of his observation of the world as experienced. The opening articles also demonstrate how Agee's life, plans for the criticism of culture, and his writing developed because he loved both life and art. The second section focuses on the accomplishment and some of the techniques of *Let Us Now Praise Famous Men*, his most extended experiment in observation. In the third section, the film criticism and screenplay writing provide another way to focus on how this writer perceived the poetic reality of his world, and how he therefore saw the possibilities of art in such perception. The fourth part of the book is about how fiction grew from Agee's own memories of the earliest part of his life. Such reliance upon memory led to his best fiction about childhood and growing up in Knoxville and at the St. Andrew's School near Sewanee, in Tennessee. The fifth section of this book is about Agee's most ambitious project, the long autobiographical manuscript which was in process when he died. This section outlines the nature of that project as he must have had it in mind, and analyzes the text of the novel, as published after his death. The next section includes an analysis of *A Death in the Family* as Agee's work of art which blends elements of the urban and rural characteristics he experienced as a child. Interestingly, that book speaks to all because of its universal qualities, but Agee focuses on the particular. His final book is a success because its particulars radiate outward to connect with the archetypal patterns of all lives.

As an interrelated group of essays, these pieces demonstrate that Agee kept asking the right questions of himself and others. The result is an unusual set of accomplishments by a writer who remains impossible to categorize, and about whom many more questions will be raised. With this fact in mind I have written the concluding essay, an analysis of writing about Agee. As a survey of what has been written about him in the decades since his death this concluding essay analyzes what scholars have had to say about Agee and his writing and provides a foundation for speculating about what kinds of questions might be raised about Agee's accomplishments in the future.

Victor A. Kramer

I

The Life and Plans for Writing

A Reconciliation of Forces:
The Life and the Work

In a manuscript written in conjunction with *A Death in the Family*, James Agee (1909-1955) emphasized his realization that he had been formed in the absence of his father. Although his phrasing is ironic, there is an important truth in his insight because so many circumstances of his life did develop as a result of his father's early death. Agee's earliest years were a combination of experiences which he drew from two families: his mother's, associated with a relatively comfortable Knoxville urban setting, and his father's, in the rural community of La Follete, Tennessee. After his father's death, when Agee was six years old, he was inevitably drawn more into the circle of his mother's family and into the values associated with her, including firm Christian belief. As he matured he came to realize that had his father lived, he would surely have been different because of the productive tension provided by both parents. Agee's best-known work, the post-humously published *A Death in the Family*, grew out of his realization. Compensations, however, flowed from changes in his life brought about by his father's abrupt death. Brought closer to members of his mother's family who valued religion, education, and art (Mrs. Agee's brother, Hugh Tyler, was an artist), the child developed a strong spiritual and aesthetic sense. Agee became increasingly aware of the importance of such facts in later years.

Agee's first eight years were spent in Knoxville; however, in 1918, just two years after his father's death in an automobile accident, his mother decided to enroll him in St. Andrew's School near Sewanee, Tennessee. He remained there through 1924, and those years proved valuable. During this period the child developed a strong appreciation of the Anglo-Catholic Church and came to know Father James Harold Flye, a history teacher at the school and a man who became his life-long friend. After Agee died, Father Flye gathered letters, written to him over a thirty-year period, and published them under the title *Letters of James Agee to Father Flye* (1962).[1] This collection is useful as an overview of Agee's life and as a testament of his affection for Father Flye. These letters provide a succinct introduction to Agee and his writing because they manifest the tension that was always present in his life, tension caused by a desire to live to the fullest and an equally compelling desire to be a great artist. Some critics have argued that Agee never resolved that tension. If this is true the tension was a positive force, for he was able to produce a large amount of work within many categories—poetry, autobiography, criticism, screenplays, and articles.

In the earliest letters to Father Flye, Agee's hope to be a writer is evident, and during that period, when he was only sixteen or seventeen years old, he demonstrated his wide range of interests—books, music, visual art, movies, language, education, religion, popular culture, psychology. Clearly, Agee sensed early that he would probably not be content to pursue a single set of interests. This fact is indicative of some of the difficulties he would later face as a writer who could always imagine an enormous variety of worthwhile projects. From his earliest years when he was ambitious and wrote prolifically, until the very end of his life, he found it difficult to decide which project to choose. Agee constantly sought ways to reconcile forces within himself that almost seemed to promise too much.

It is only speculation, but not without a basis in fact, that Agee's mother might have chosen St. Andrew's, a boarding school run by the monastic order of the Holy Cross of the Episcopal Church, to curb his impulsiveness and enthusiasm. She must have sensed that the young boy would profit from the rigor of religious teachers who would provide guidance in the absence of a father, and according to Father Flye, one of the reasons Mrs. Agee chose St. Andrew's was the presence of male teachers on the faculty of that isolated mountain school.[2] It is significant that Agee's mother did not return to Knoxville, but instead took up residence adjacent to the school grounds. Passages Agee wrote for *The Morning Watch* approximately a quarter century later make clear that the atmosphere of the school was important for young Agee, yet it was an atmosphere qualified by his mother's proximity. She too had found a place which was satisfying aesthetically and religiously. Such associations remained important for both mother and son throughout their lives. Although Agee drifted away from formal connections with the Church in his adult life, his Christian belief always remained important. This influence can be seen in all his major writings, as well as in his contribution to the *Partisan Review* symposium "Religion and the Intellectuals" (1950) which emphasizes a continuing attempt to accommodate natural and supernatural impulses.[3]

By the time Agee was ready to leave St. Andrew's in 1924, much of his attachment to belief and ritual in the Anglo-Catholic Church had been formed. At that time, when he was about fourteen years old, he had not yet decided to be a writer. The following year, he returned to Knoxville for a year of high school before enrolling at the Phillips Exeter Academy. During the summer of 1925 he and Father Flye traveled in Europe, and during that trip Agee first expressed an interest in writing. In the three years that followed, the incipient literary career began to unfold. Agee wrote in large quantity and a considerable amount was published in *The Phillips Exeter Monthly*. In his earliest sketches, some of which are based on what he had seen in France, Agee already sought to go beyond fiction and document a world observed.[4] A careful reading of his Exeter writings reveals an eye for detail that also characterizes much subsequent writing—articles, poetry, and autobiography. Just as early, his primary interest was to focus upon the immediacy of the particular, fundamentally, Agee's entire career can be described as a continuing attempt to reconcile his intense appreciation of life with a desire to express a vision of life in language (or film). Finally, Agee would acknowledge the inability of words to express fully the dignity of life, but he also knew that attempts to reconcile such forces were at the heart of what he always did best as a writer.

The early literary productions published in the *Exeter Monthly* include fiction, poetry, drama, and reviews. That material, never edited for republication, sets a tone and pace for the varied career which followed. Agee was never content to work quietly in one safe haven of a writer's calling. This earliest literary work is often derivative, yet the variety of the fiction, satire, drama, and poetry published at Exeter from November 1925 to June 1928 clearly demonstrates success with what later became both help and hindrance—a stubborn insistence on nonspecialization. Within this earliest work is exhibited his penchant for careful observation, wit, and irony. For example, his story "Knoxville High" seems to be based on memories of the year he spent in Knoxville in 1924-1925 and satirizes small-town provincialism. This humorous story is an experiment with stream-of-consciousness. Other stories with Tennessee settings are sometimes somber, but are quite tightly executed. "The Circle," which seems to have been influenced by Sherwood Anderson, is about a young man trapped by his father's death. Still others of these earliest stories reflect wide reading and a thorough knowledge of classical literature.

Another important work is the manuscript poem "Pygmalion," probably the same piece Agee mentions in a letter to Father Flye in 1928. "Pygmalion" is a sustained example of early abilities and an objectification of doubts about what artists accomplish. While this early work cannot be dated exactly, it is significant because much of his later literary career involved devising methods that would reflect a personal vision of actuality. Many of his best works are attempts to catch the texture of ordinary life, and his classic documentary *Let Us Now Praise Famous Men* is largely about the impossibility of communicating what has been experienced. A similar problem is central to "Pygmalion," a soliloquy spoken by the Creator, who describes his inception, formation, and destruction of a world, his "glorious dreams."[5] In the young artist's imagination the world seems so beautiful that the Creator must "strain" to alleviate His agony, yet such a magnificent caress results in a "bruised and broken" world. "Pygmalion" demonstrates that early in his career Agee was struggling with questions about appropriate artistic form; and just a few years later, during the 1930s, he was to find it increasingly difficult to rely upon a traditional framework, either of Christian thought or of a conventional poetic form. This is already evident in work he accomplished while a student at Harvard.

Agee's apprentice writing published in *The Harvard Advocate* included poetry, fiction, and reviews written over a four-year period, 1928-1932; during his senior year he was editor of the *Advocate*. The twenty-six poems written for *The Harvard Advocate* illustrate the manner in which Agee assimilated traditional writers. Almost all of these poems appear in *The Collected Poems* but only eight of the Harvard poems were included in Agee's first book, *Permit Me Voyage,* seven as revisions for a sonnet sequence. Much more important for illustrating Agee's development is the undergraduate prose. Fitzgerald states that the Harvard poetry never seemed to possess the rhythm and power of the fiction.[6] The prose is powerful because it reflects Agee's convictions about the difficulty of good writing. One can separate the undergraduate prose into two groups: stories that rely heavily on imagination and others that grow out of personal experience, or at least are limited to experiences someone as young as Agee could adequately present. "Boys Will Be Brutes," about the slaughter of tiny birds taken from their nest, is successful because its apparent basis is clearly an actual, or a believably portrayed, experience.

The writing completed at Harvard indicates that Agee early mastered conventional modes of writing. Two things about his undergraduate writing are especially significant: he was at ease with standard forms while he was continually seeking to develop new ways of writing. The story "They That Sow in Sorrow Shall Reap" is therefore an example of a story that suggests states of consciousness as ideas flow from one person to another. Throughout the story Agee is able to suggest consciousness by focusing upon things observed. A completely different example is Agee's skillful engineering of a parody of an issue of *Time* magazine, an exercise that helped him secure a job as a writer for *Fortune* after he left Harvard. These two types of writing, an experimental attempt to suggest the complexity of individual consciousness and a humorous parody of a news magazine, suggest the range of Agee's ability.

It is clear that throughout his Harvard years and into the 1930s Agee sought to develop new ways of writing. These attempts account for his interest in a Byronic experiment, "John Carter," which he began at Harvard, as well as for the accomplishment and frustration of much of his writing for *Fortune*. Both the long poem and the unsigned articles reflect a fundamental division that remained within him as a writer. When he graduated from Harvard and began writing for *Fortune* in 1932, he was surely happy to have a job. But he had taken the position at *Fortune* with no intention of staying; during his first year there he applied for a Guggenheim Fellowship. One of the projects he hoped to finish was the long poem, "John Carter," a work which was, in his words, to be "a complete appraisal of contemporary civilization, and a study of the Problem of Evil." This poem is as ambitious as *Famous Men*. Agee's satire attacks a society that has lost reverence for tradition; "John Carter" emphasizes the hypocrisy that informs what passes for religion and art.

During these early years, while he was supporting himself as a journalist, Agee was also distancing himself from much of what was held to be of value in conventional journalism and poetry; an unpublished essay about his first published book emphasizes this separation. Agee's book of poetry had appeared in the Yale Series of Younger Poets, and a more conventional "young poet" might have been content to express gratitude that his poetry had been chosen for such a prestigious series. The unpublished essay is significant because it clearly demonstrates his ambivalent attitude toward *Permit Me Voyage* (1934). Agee wrote the essay as if he were reviewing the volume; essentially he suggested that *Permit Me Voyage* stands as a record of things accomplished but also as a record of ventures that he did not want to repeat. His dissatisfaction also clarifies how and why he chose to write as he did in the decades which followed. Two of his comments are of special value because they demonstate what he had accomplished and show how he was ready to go one step further.

> Putting the ms. together in the first place was a good deal of trouble. I had the poems and verses in many lengths and tones: all put together they would not only burst the requisite limit of the volume; they would jangle more than even I could care for. I had for instance the first chunks of a long, loose, obscene, satirical, moral, dramatic-narrative, metaphysical, lyrical poem ["John Carter"] which, were I to let it loose at this time, would knock your eye out. . . .
>
> One of the heaviest problems and contradictions within me is that of the human being vs the artist. Which resolves itself, ultimately, into the Battle of the Centuries: God vs Art. Granted that they can be neck and neck, and granted that they breed as well as murder one another, I am finally in favour of art, and I believe that in ways and for reasons, which I shall not enter upon here, they are the same. Yet their struggle is violent enough to blow the brain where it goes on. In the interests of such truths as I was able to apprehend, it was therefore inevitable that both kinds of poetry should go into this volume.[7]

Other parts of his "reflections" provide additional comments about specific parts of the book, its "derivative" faults, and its ambitious innovations. In some ways Agee's attitude about this first book seems to be similar to his attitude as a journalist. Both conventional poetry and formal journalism could be accomplished, but they seemed "crystallized," and while he could produce such facile work, he really wanted to concentrate on "his own writing."

Agee's "Plans for Work," which accompanied a second application for a Guggenheim in October 1937, indicates how passionately he was interested in writing. The application must have seemed quite odd to the selection committee. Included was an elaborate outline for forty-seven proposed projects, and predictably, no fellowship was forthcoming. Agee explained how he planned to do various pieces of fiction, in addition to notes on photography, music, theater, and revues. Five of his proposals were suggestions for fiction, but he also wished to write serious stories "whose whole intention is the direct communication of the intensity of common experience." Other proposals contained outlines for various analyses, poems, and collections of data. Agee was clearly fascinated with the possibilities the ordinary world offered for analysis and as a challenge to communication.[8]

Much of what he actually accomplished in the 1930s and later is an extension of his fascination with the complexity of ordinary emotion and consciousness. An unpublished story, "Before God and This Company" (1939), a draft for a piece never finished, stands as a further example of how he sought to use an analytical journalistic method to record the "commonplace" events that surrounded him.[9] Agee's subject is marital love, and interestingly these were years when his marriage to Via Saunders ended in divorce, and only a few years later a second marriage to Alma Mailman also disintegrated. In method, the sketch foreshadows the concentration of detail basic to *Let Us Now Praise Famous Men*, a manuscript probably in process when the sketch was written. Agee's draft matter-of-factly records specific events during a Saturday night party. Couples fight and talk, and people go about their business barely aware that their actions affect others.

Let Us Now Praise Famous Men (1941) has been described in innumerable ways—and it is finally *the* documentary that surpasses others of that genre. Agee knew it was impossible to catch the "*uni*-magined," but he knew this was a chance to document what he had lived. Critics sometimes assert that the presence of Agee's tortured consciousness makes his text too personal. However, he knew that there was no way for him to be both honest and "objective," and such a realization accounts for the success of this unusual text. In large part Agee's text is a parody of the very type of journalism that had probably frustrated him from 1933 through 1939. In *Famous Men*, we see his awareness of the journalistic constrictions that had sent him South to observe a "typical" farm family. He had been told to get facts, but in realization of that impossibility, he sought to inundate editors and readers with facts. Through this technique, he reveals his doubts about stock assumptions, and the text becomes, among other things, a condemnation of those who confidently think they might get at the essence of reality through language.

Almost predictably, when *Famous Men* was published in 1941, no one seemed particularly interested in Agee's experiment in communication. His method of reporting, in gestation for years, finally included the total experience. The writer's confrontation with myriad distortions is at the heart of the book. A fundamental assumption undergirding the text—ironically a work of "Art," despite Agee's insistence that it is not—is that any attempt to provide an accurate record of what is observed is doomed. The basic notion to be communicated was that while distinct persons and events were apprehended, Agee knew that he too had been definitely affected by what was experienced, and *his* reactions were equally important. *Famous Men's* aesthetic, therefore, focuses attention on details as remembered, but modified by the writer's reflection. Agee knew that what he experienced could never be fully communicated; he even says that, if it were possible, there would be "no writing at all."[10] His insistence on being present throughout *Famous Men* violates accepted criteria for journalism and documentaries, as well as for Art. A section-by-section analysis of his text reveals how he voices questions about what he is doing.

In part two of his text, which provides "Findings and Comments," Agee writes about money, shelter, clothing, education, and work. His method emphasizes divisions within his mind. He clearly respects language and uses it carefully, but simultaneously he doubts the success of ever communicating the essence of what he has experienced. Agee realized that much could be implied about his Alabama experience. He also hoped that *Famous Men* was only a beginning, perhaps the first of several volumes. His "Work" chapter demonstrates his success with expansion of this material. Unpublished notebook material also indicates that he seriously thought about using the techniques he had developed for *Famous Men* in analogous projects.[11] In a sense his film criticism became that analysis.

Examination of the numerous book reviews he wrote between 1939 and 1942 reveals how his career developed as his skills as an observer developed. Through the experience of writing *Famous Men*, reviewing books and movies, and becoming increasingly analytical about the culture as a whole, Agee was gradually perfecting skills that allowed him to reconcile at least some of his great affection for the world with analysis and evocation of that world. He wrote one hundred reviews for *Time*, covering a wide range of books. Each reviewer could choose what he would review, and Agee's method was akin to that he later refined for the movie criticism—always seeking ways to relate the work to wider movements within the culture.

An examination of the many stories Agee wrote for *Time*, both published and unpublished, also reveals how he systematically sought to provide analysis of a culture which, he feared, had in some fundamental ways become lost. Two rejected pieces about popular culture, medicine deemed too strong for publication in the mass-circulation magazine, reflect Agee's increasing concern that "the world's history, and the daily and future destiny of every individual, are given shape, by the thousands of great and trivial assumptions, taboos, fears, prejudices, which men in effective numbers believe so fully that they act accordingly."[12] The malformed opinions Agee listed ranged from views about the "nobleness" of war and "democracy" to the conviction that groups and races can be guilty as groups or races or that it is possible "to enjoy the benefits of materialism without being liable to its hazards." Such "beliefs" were, he feared, what really caused people to act. Seldom did they act out of personal conviction or religious belief. More often than not, they simply adopted the thoughts of others and other groups. Other manuscript materials outline projects Agee hoped to accomplish by standing back from the culture as a whole. One is a long outline of a proposed evaluation of culture; those ideas could even today become a model for intelligent criticism of a nonreflective society.[13] Another manuscript, a letter written as a preface to a statement of eighteen pages to Archibald MacLeish, then Librarian of Congress, is about a project to preserve films as examples of the best (and worst) the culture had generated. Insights from these manuscripts help us to understand Agee's critical procedure and his mature creative works.

As has been established, Agee's career was always a combination of impulses that reflected a wish to live well and to be a successful writer. Yet as he lived through World War II and its aftermath, he came to feel that it was getting harder and harder for individuals to act responsibly. Such a realization increasingly influenced much of his mature writing. His personal convictions about the difficulty of acting as an individual were intensified by the horrors of the atomic bomb; in his opinion the war, and the cynicism connected with it, had been too easily accepted. His most succinct literary treatment of the demise of individualism is the satire "Dedication Day, a Rough Sketch for a Motion Picture," which satirizes an imagined dedication of a monument to the discovery of the atom's destructive power. The partly autobiographical "1928 Story" also grows out of related thinking and foreshadows later autobiographical fiction.[14] "1928 Story" catches the spontaneity and enthusiasm of an earlier time in Agee's life and corroborates significant facts about him as a mature writer. It is the first sustained attempt after *Famous Men* to recreate a time from his own life. As this story opens, Irvine, a writer, listens to old records that remind him of happier years when the same music was heard in an altogether more hopeful atmosphere. The story, like *The Morning Watch*, is a step toward *A Death in the Family* and shows how Agee learned to focus on the particularities of his own life. Thus, while the story begins with a mood of frustration and disappointment, Agee refines those emotions into the art of remembrance. An interesting point, therefore, is that just as *Famous Men* grew out of a journalism assignment for *Fortune*, the final fiction was, to some degree, the result of frustrations experienced during years as a journalist and writer in New York City ten years later. "1928 Story" might therefore be thought of as a preliminary exercise for *The Morning Watch* (1950) and *A Death in the Family*.

In *The Morning Watch* Agree returns to memories of St. Andrew's two decades earlier to evoke a high point of religious experience for a twelve-year-old boy. The novella takes place during the early hours of Maundy Thursday and celebrates his experiences. Fictionalized and heightened, Agee's account becomes far more than a record of a few hours on a religious day. It is a celebration of the mystery of living developed through the awareness of the main character, Richard, of developing strengths, biological and aesthetic, that impinge upon a religious sensibility.

Agee's most famous autobiographical work is *A Death in the Family*, a novel which was incomplete at his death. He probably began work on this book late in the 1940s (at approximately the same time as he wrote "1928 Story"). His marriage to Mia Fritsch and the promise of a family of his own may have triggered his desire to fictionalize his own childhood. Possibly the writing of a successful Omnibus television series about the life of Abraham Lincoln reminded him of his father. The fictional Jay is compared to Lincoln in the novel. More than likely Agee's sense of his own impending death as he approached age forty and felt he had not accomplished as much as he had wished sent his imagination back to these earlier years.

A *Death in the Family* is an unusual novel because it is both a detailed remembrance of specifics and an archetypal depiction of events within any family. It is a book about marital love and loss, about initiation of children into life, and about maturation and loss for adults. It is a book about religious faith and the need for religion. It is a book about the urban and rural conflict so many Americans have experienced in this century. Yet, while it is all of these things, it is Agee's specific documentation of his life when he was four, five, and six years old. The book is a demonstration of how art can be produced from the tension of a changing world.

Still another example of Agee's creative response to problems observed in his contemporary world is a screenplay he hoped to do for Charlie Chaplin. This working draft, "Scientists and Tramps," included sketches for many scenes.[15] Some dialogue was projected; several scenes were outlined; the prologue was worked out in detail. The prologue was to be composed of newsreel clips and accompanied by a satirical speech. Its opening harangue of democracy, given by a "Grand Old Man," is a beautiful example of parody, which Agee relished. The speech illustrates what occurs if people pretend they are individuals when they are only members of an unthinking herd. This screenplay was only sketched, yet the extant notes provide insight into many aspects of Agee's final years as a scenario writer. His recognition as a screenwriter began in the late 1940s with *The Quiet One*, a documentary about a boy from Harlem who is sent to a correctional institution. Agee suggested that city streets be used in this film and that nonactors be employed to catch the reality of that city. Also, he foresaw that continuous dialogue would not be necessary.[16] All of these elements have combined to make this film a classic. Much additional successful screen work followed, including the adaptation of works by various fiction writers. Five of Agee's screenplays are included in *Agee on Film*, volume two.

Agee's career produced a varied corpus, but the nine books he left are of value because in all his projects he sought and found ways to honor the life he loved. Whether in poetry or for the screen, whether in journalism or in fiction, he found ways to evoke actuality. Through art, which creates new moments, he gives us glimpses of a constantly changing world.

Notes

[1] *Letters of James Agee to Father Flye,* edited by James Harold Flye (New York: George Braziller, 1962). The second edition of this book contains a new preface and additional letters of Father Flye to Agee (Boston: Houghton Mifflin Company, 1971).

[2] Interview with Father James Harold Flye, New York City, 29 December 1968.

[3] "Religion and the Intellectuals," *Partisan Review* 17 (February 1950):106-113.

[4] Various stories and sketches published in *The Phillips Exeter Monthly* are based on the trip to Europe. See, for example, "The Scar," 30 (January 1926).

[5] The complete text of "Pygmalion" has been edited. See my "Agee's Early Poem 'Pygmalion' and His Aesthetic," *Mississippi Quarterly* 29 (Spring 1976):191-196.

[6] Two of Agee's best Harvard stories are in *The Collected Short Prose of James Agee* (Boston: Houghton Mifflin Company, 1968). See "Death in the Desert" and "They That Sow in Sorrow Shall Reap," 61-75 and 75-98.

[7] "Reflections on *Permit Me Voyage.*" Typescript, Humanities Research Center, The University of Texas at Austin Library. The kind permission of the James Agee Trust has been granted for use of selected quotations from this and other manuscripts used throughout this essay.

[8] See *The Collected Short Prose of James Agee* (Boston: Houghton Mifflin Company, 1968) 131-148.

[9] "Before God and This Company, or Bigger Than We Are." Pencil Manuscript. Humanities Research Center.

[10] *Let Us Now Praise Famous Men* (Boston: Houghton Mifflin Company, 1941) 13. All subsequent quotations for *Famous Men* are noted parenthetically.

[11] The complete "Work" chapter has been edited. See my article and text in *The Texas Quarterly* 15 (Summer 1972):27-48.

[12] "Consider the lilies. . . ." Typescript. Humanities Research Center.

[13] "Notes and Suggestions on the magazine under discussion." Humanities Research Center.

[14] "1928 Story" has been edited. It is part of a special section of *The Texas*

Quarterly 11 (1968). See my "Agee's Struggle To Be a Writer" within the section entitled "Agee in the Forties," 9-55.

[15] "Scientists and Tramps" is catalogued "Unidentified television or screenplay." Autograph manuscript working draft with autograph revisions (62 pp.). Humanities Research Center.

[16] Details of Agee's writing for *The Quiet One* can be observed in the manuscript materials available for this scenario catalogued as "Wiltwyck Movie." Humanities Research Center.

Criticism of Culture as a Basic Thrust

James Agee was capable of devising many different, and often unfinishable, projects; and while he accomplished many of his goals, some of these tasks never came to fruition. One of his hopes remains applicable today, perhaps more so than when, over forty years ago, he first argued for some form of its implementation. Agee realized the need for a new type of analysis to be concerned primarily with facets of popular culture which routinely go unquestioned in contemporary American society. He saw that a regular outlet, perhaps a magazine, might be developed. Its primary function would be the scrutiny of words and images as they are employed in everyday contexts. With the electronic age a fact, and individualism more threatened than ever before, even partial implementation of Agee's suggestions could still have import.

At several different times he proposed a magazine (or perhaps a continuing series of books) for the criticism of popular culture. His enthusiasm for what would have had to be an extended, and admittedly herculean chore, probably was received by his associates in the nineteen-thirties and forties with about as much excitement as was his final projected screenplay, a fantasy about man's captivity of elephants which he described in an unposted letter to Father Flye. In that letter Agee mentioned his plans for the elephant screenplay, and added, "Almost nobody I've described it to likes this idea, except me. It has its weaknesses, but I like it."[1] That projected film would have been about man's cruelty and stupidity toward elephants. One can be sure that a similar exuberance must have gone into Agee's projections for the development of a method of analysis of the everyday reality of how man reveals himself. No fantasy would be necessary to perceive the cruelty and stupidity of contemporary man; this is daily revealed in his actions and speech and use of the printed word.

The problem was how to make men aware of their misuses of

both language and image. Agee knew that a careful appraisal of what might not be even noticed as unusual would be as fascinating and as revealing as any study of a work of "art."[2] But in addition such analysis could be of benefit to others because it might make them aware of incongruities before unnoticed. Thus in letters to friends, in enthusiastic memoranda to editors, in a beautiful (and unsuccessful) Guggenheim application in 1937, and in scattered notes, Agee articulated his hopes for such a critical project—or a series of them. His ideas have their basis in the development of procedures which would allow new stories, advertisements, public speeches, private letters, movies, etc.— often accepted as correct, or right, or factual—to be subjected to a critical assessment like that which editorials in newspaper begin to provide for certain public issues.

Of course he realized that this scheme would have to be a seriously developed project built on a continuing basis. An adequate staff and patronage would have been absolutely essential. Whether such a project was workable as originally proposed is questionable. His hopes were for a project which would finally require several persons (and considerable funds) to be sustained.

The ideas which he espoused are certainly not completely original with him. New approaches to criticism, and a developing concern with the "lively" arts were part of the atmosphere of the twenties and thirties when Agee was coming of age. As an undergraduate he had met with and was fascinated by the ideas of I. A. Richards. And it is somewhat ironic to recall that Agee's initial position, as a staff writer at *Fortune* magazine, secured during the height of the depression in 1932, was attained, at least partly because of a successful parody of *Time* magazine which he helped engineer as an editor of *The Harvard Advocate*.

In 1937 he called one facet of what he had in mind "Hung with their own rope."[3] He felt no one word covered what he meant, but the material was "abundant." His idea was "that the self-deceived and corrupted betray themselves and their world more definitively than invented satire can." Examples: Eleanor Roosevelt's syndicated newspaper column *My Day*; court records; editorials; "the 'literature' concerning and justifying the castration of Eisenstein"; etc. Such material, he felt, might well be simply "exhibited" in a book or magazine. And while no extended project like this was ever accomplished, much of Agee's later writing incorporates facets of what he realized could be done.

His *Let Us Now Praise Famous Men* is, among other things, an attempt to represent the real world; yet because of the difficulty of what was attempted in that work, its text finally stands as a document with its ostensible subject a study of tenant farming, while just as important a subject is the inquiry into the impossibility of any true communication because Agee knew and admitted it was impossible to give the texture of what had been experienced. One thing he did know as he wrote that text: it was the merest beginning, only a gesture (however elaborate) which reflected the difficulty of recording and communicating accurately any *un*imagined part of existence.

One of the most important things accomplished in *Famous Men* is that the text stands as an honest attempt to deal with the difficulty (in fact, the impossibility) of communicating about the true nature of reality. Agee's complicated development of technique within that book illustrates how a complex subject experienced, recalled, remembered, and imagined had to be approached in several different ways. One recalls one of his prefatory statements about *Famous Men*:

> If I could do it, I'd do no writing at all here. It would be
> photographs; the rest would be fragments of cloth, bits of
> cotton, lumps of earth, records of speech, pieces of wood
> and iron, phials of odors, plates of food and of excrement.[4]

In notes which were apparently composed as he wrote a revision of *Famous Men*'s "Preamble," he outlined plans for a series of periodicals, the point of which would be, he wrote, "a hardness of standard, and lack of concession, nowhere else to be found in American publishing."[5] But these periodicals were to be different in kind from anything else published. The notes project a "series" (perhaps volumes?) "edited by W. E. [Walker Evans] and J. A. " The "general content" was to have been "some text, some pictures. Records, symbols, scenic analysis and criticism." Some of the subjects listed were the following: "Travelling in America: text and photographs, 60 days travelling: as exactly as possible recorded and analyzed"; "an attack on the M of M [Museum of Modern?] Art"; a study of "motion pictures as caught midway in becoming respectable." Each of these projected studies would have focused on an aspect of the culture as it revealed itself.

Other subjects which were listed as possibilities included these:

> An exposition of methods by which corruption betrays
> itself.
> A sampling of letters.
> A sampling of news and magazine clips.
> Series: poems: composed of advertisements, news photo-
> graphs personally made. . . .
> A record and analysis of one week's work on *Time*. . . .

This series, of course, also never developed. But Agee's interest in such subjects was to continue. His introductions to volumes of photographs by both Walker Evans and Helen Levitt are the natural outgrowth of an aesthetic vision which has its basis in an apprehension of the real world.

Agee's letters are also sprinkled with references to aspects of an everyday world that demanded analysis. And in 1944 he wrote an article entitled "Pseudo-Folk," in which he illustrated the complexity of our culture's confusion when different levels of experience blend together, while those who are participants in the culture remain unaware of the mutations which have taken place. There he wrote that "the quintessence of this special kind of vicious psuedo-folk [was] Hazel Scott. She plays the sort of jazz one could probably pick up, by now, through a correspondence school. She plays her 'classics' with a slobbering, anarchic, vindictive, rushing affectation which any mediocre elementary piano teacher would slap her silly for."[6]

Agee is inattentive to the fact that the reflectiveness which his ideas call for is in conflict with the irreflective quality of much popular culture. Apparently he did not think much about the distinction between making judgments about aspects of culture and the fact that such reflection would be isolated from the thing under scrutiny. This problem suggests the difficulty of what he hoped to accomplish.

In other places, such as in the caustic satire "Dedication Day" (1946) Agee satirized a society which forgets how to criticize itself. That satire, a sketch for a motion picture, but also a parody of a news story, is about the elaborately developed dedicatory ceremonies for a monument commemorating man's first horrid use of atomic energy.

It is certainly not surprising that when Agee began to write film criticism for *The Nation* in 1941 he immediately indicated how he felt as an "amateur" who had assumed the task of reviewing the complexity of cinema. He did not feel his "amateur" status was a handicap. That unprofessional status allowed him the freedom to react as an individual. In his initial column he included paragraphs elaborating his doubts about the screen version of *The Grapes of Wrath* (a subject which had also rated commentary in the notebook mentioned earlier about a projected series dealing with aspects of popular culture). The truth which Steinbeck had attempted to reveal was too much distorted through the making of a movie, and this problem is compounded when such a film is disguised as "reality." Also in an early column doubts about whether war atrocity films could ever in conscience be viewed were elaborated. His concern in both instances is that when "reality" is at the heart of a film, it must be honored, or the result can only be a betrayal of what is real, and of what it is possible both for the motion picture to reflect and distort.

Agee's film criticism, a major recipient of his energies through-out the forties, is in fact, the practice of the kind of analysis he knew might be applied to other cultural forms, but restricted to only one aspect of America's culture. That criticism provides a *modus operandi* for an approach which might be applied to many other aspects of a culture which often go unquestioned. A basic ingredient in the criticism is a constant recognition that the banal, even the deceitful, as well as poetic and honest attempts to mirror reality, are all equally indicative of our culture. Finally they are revealing as the most complex kind of dream. Agee's comments on *The Blue Dahlia* (1946) are, I think, typical of an ability to see in films values which probably even their makers were unaware of. He said he hoped

> there will be more films of the quality of *The Blue Dahlia*, rather than fewer. The picture is as neatly stylized and synchronized, and as uninterested in moral excitement, as a good ballet; it knows its own weight and size perfectly and carries them gracefully and without self-importance; it is, barring occasional victories and noble accidents, about as good a movie as can be expected from the big factories. In its own uninsistent way, for that matter, it does carry a certain amount of social criticism. For it crawls with American types; and their mannerisms and affectations, and their chief preoccupations—blackmail and what's-in-it-for-me—all seem to me to reflect, however coolly, things that are deeply characteristic of this civilization.[7]

Such criticism alerts a viewer to notice aspects of a film which otherwise might be overlooked.

Throughout his criticism Agee weighs the merits of contemporary movies, both for what they accomplish as films and also for the ways they reveal the culture. Thus, artifice imposed by a Hollywood film which denatures reality; or the use of newsreel clips within the wrong context of a fiction film; or the use of professional actors when amateurs could have been better employed, often become the objects of Agee's scrutiny.

He was sure much could be revealed by study of little if one looked carefully at what is not usually observed. For such reasons he saw value in simply preserving the ordinary or commonplace in both verbal and pictorial record. Without comment or editing, the commonplace reveals when it is properly beheld. Agee was once asked to recommend a group of films which might be worth preserving for a film library. He wrote extensive notes, and as one might expect, he was as enthusiastic about the mediocre, as about the good films. He wrote pages and pages about films which were produced only for grade "B" distribution and maximum economic return.[8] He saw that it was precisely in the "ordinary" film that one could see the essence of a culture revealed. In many places in his film criticism he suggests that most films are a variety of anthropological data. So even the most obviously commercial film can be a means for revealing aspects of society. Properly observed it will reveal all manner of things about the culture.

In a related manner, Agee realized that much of what makes up ordinary "thinking" was, in fact, not thinking at all—but rather a reliance upon a series of cliches and half-truths which the public then comes to assume possesses truth. He prepared an article (for *Time*?) which had the title "Popular Religion."[9] There he elaborated upon the fact that much of what men in the United States believe (with an almost religious fervor) is merely an amalgam of ideas assimilated, but with little basis in truth. Thus during the Second World War, he noted, most Americans simply assumed all Germans were beasts.

Sometimes in the mid nineteen-forties, while still a working journalist, Agee drafted suggestions in which he proposed a new department for *Time* magazine. He labeled this proposed new section "Double-Take"; and suggested photographs, public speeches, and advertising might all be subject to a special kind of analysis. He noted advertising is, I feel sure, as thoroughly worth reviewing as [theatre, books, movies,] are: it seems to me a singularly edged and intricate crystallization of a little that is passable and a great deal that is not, among most of the minds, beliefs, emotions and motives of the country.[10]

He then included an elaborate analysis of an ad by "a natural gas transmission company," to which he appended "Natural gas, indeed!" After he had provided examples of an inadvertent self-indictment by the gas people (part of the copy, unfortunately, had read "Some day peace must fall on a world.") he noted that at first "the full, strange, subconscious, polysemantic horror of *must fall on* rather amused me rather nastily instead of appalling me." His point of course is that other readers might not have been amused; and that the incongruity of inappropriate uses of language such as those chosen by this copywriter were worth notice. What fascinated him was the realization that myriads of possibilities offered themselves for analysis throughout the culture as a whole, but that most of what is popularly accepted is never understood. And because understanding is lacking, the potential within the culture is usually not fulfilled. If even some of these things could be analyzed, dissected, and criticized, then perhaps steps could be taken toward providing insights which would lead to better appreciation of the potentialities which the culture possessed. This is to say that Agee knew that so much of what is accepted without question in our society is finally dehumanizing. To make men aware of how they participate in their own dehumanization would be a necessary first step toward any rectification.

Agee noted that a "Double-Take" enterprise would not have to be limited to "self-betrayals in print." Those in "unpublished living," are just as revelatory, and are "abundant for collection," he noted. One way to provide access to such materials would be simply to print "the unconsciously naked sentence, given either with or without context." When Agee suggests that inadvertent slips of phrase or pen are revealing, he is, of course, relying upon a procedure different from criticism. What he suggests is akin to psychoanalysis.

For related reasons he was vitally interested in the value of personal letters throughout his career. This fascination with letters suggests what he realized could be seen in all artifacts, and uses of language. But letters are "as distinct in their own way, and as valuable, as would be a faultless record of the dreams of many individuals. All letters have an immediacy and a flawlessness unvariable in any other written form."[11] And thus he hoped for the possibility of collections of letters published without analysis; and as well he saw the need, and use for "an almost word by word analysis . . . as many sided and extensive as the given letter requires." Only two months after the 1939 manuscript for *Famous Men* was finished Agee had written Father Flye to ask if he would be willing for some of his letters to be used in a proposed collection of letters which he, and two others, were discussing.[12] Mention of the value of personal letters continues to recur throughout the forties.

Agee's most extended description of a method which might have been developed to incorporate many of his ideas about the criticism of popular culture is an eight page statement written by him in the mid-1940's. That statement ("Notes and Suggestions on the magazine under discussion") outlines his proposed stance for a new type of journal. While admitting that the very highest critical standards should be maintained for the inclusion of fiction and satire, he admitted that if such standards were consistently followed there would be an "apparent gap in materials available for inclusion." That gap could be filled "in a way that no magazine or other publication so far as he knew attempts to fill." His words capsulize his hopes:

> It is the business of journalism to report; of comment and analysis it does very little. . . . Nominally editors, columists, etc. make comment and analysis their business; but the results are almost without exception that the mere surface has been scraped. . . . I suggest that this proposed magazine could work a pincer-movement on experience or "reality," with journalism functioning very importantly as a part of the opposite arm of the pincers. We would use the findings of journalists, in other words, as they in turn use the findings of researches; we can also supplement or extend their reporting by direct investigations. . . .
>
> This section of the magazine would be subdivided into many others, and would constitute a complete review, analysis and documentation of what has been happening in fields which are not, normally, under very strict review . . . our technique of review would be quite untraditional; we would, in fact, have to invent it. A best seller, for instance, should be reviewed not only on its "entertainment value"; we should investigate the causes of that particular "value": and we should treat it, chiefly, as the

valuably suggestive anthropological exhibit which it essentially is.[13]

Thus, a new kind of "criticism" would be developed, and it might assist
readers to understand why particular items in a culture are, or are not,
held in esteem. In addition, an explanation of why, or how, taste
changes at different times would become part of the analysis. A work
under scrutiny would not be analyzed just as a separate entity, but in
relation to other aspects of the culture too.

Agee listed and sketched over a dozen separate categories or
possible "departments" for this proposed magazine. In some instances
he even named specific persons who he felt were best qualified for a
particular kind of criticism. Advertising art and copy; moving pictures; music; books, public speeches; letters; records; art as well as
rather more specialized areas like "sexual ethics" were included.

In these plans he included a category labeled "self-criticism."
Self-attack and analysis and "disagreement among its editors" would
be necessary if the enterprise was to be a success. Agee knew "it
is hard enough for one man to hold to the standards we are presuma-
bly setting; far harder for a group to do so; the only possible development and continuance of health is in a wide-open self and mutual-
criticism."

One of the things which he hoped might be accomplished by
such a magazine would have been "to undeceive readers of their
own—and the editors'—conditioned reflexes." Agee added the qualification that poorly run such an endeavor could be "one of the most
vicious things that has ever seen print." Essential to his doubts was the
question

> whether "popularization" is intrinsically diseased and self-
> defeating [,] or extrinsically [diseased, because most popu-
> larizers are primarily interested in their pocketbooks]. It
> might be possible for instance to contrive techniques for
> making clear to the most average reader—gradually—
> what is true and what is phoney in a photograph or a public
> speech or a letter; [sic] without sacrificing or in the long run
> simplifying any standard or perception we have. But if we
> judge it impossible, then we must by no means try any
> "next-best thing"; for every next-best thing is worst.

Ultimately what he outlined in these notes was a special kind of criticism which already, he said, a very small minority of sophisticated readers ("which . . . read *The Dial* or *Criterion* or *Kenyon Review*") used to a small extent in their conversation and in letters, but which "has been used in print little if at all." This many faceted magazine which Agee dreamed of never materialized.

Agee's many suggestions imply a need for a regular medium which would analyze all manner of things. Had he been able to develop some of his projects he would have approached these undertakings (given a prodigious amount of energy and minimum support) in the same "amateur" way he had already approached the cinema.

It is a commonplace to assert that Agee valued life above "Art"; therefore, the fake, the distorted, and the hypocritical as well as the sincere and genuine were to be observed. His plans for a regular mode of approach for criticism of popular culture did not develop, but these ideas remain sensible, and they may still serve as an impetus for others to pursue. Some journals and magazines do a little of what Agee had in mind; but usually the material placed under scrutiny is either banal or esoteric. Thus a misquotation provides a filler for *The New Yorker*, and a poorly written church bulletin provides amusement for a miscellaneous column in the *National Catholic Reporter*. At the other end of the spectrum scholars shrewdly haggle about the work of other scholars. Such material would have interested Agee, but only to a small degree.

He envisaged a medium through which the culture of the day might be scrutinized. The kind of "criticism" which he hoped to see provided is, to some small degree, made available in a few programs of analysis on television—some of which follow a "magazine" format. (Variations on his suggestions for use of everyday materials for analysis are regularly pursued by teachers of writing who combine traditional rhetorical methods with an awareness of a student's world.) And in the work of men like McLuhan some of what Agee foresaw has been accomplished.

The fact that many aspects of culture do not easily lend themselves to "analysis" remains a fact. The medium is often the message; and many modern critics have become cautious about too much analysis. But at the same time those within a culture should be aware of the changes taking place within it.

Words and images just because they are words and images are not a faithful representation of reality; and dishonesty and imprecision with the very breath of man's spirit is a most grievous distortion. It is idealistic to hope that someone might employ all of Agee's ideas. But they seem a fresh approach, and could be of immense value for a society which exhibits every evidence of needing to find methods to examine it conscience systematically.[14]

Notes

[1] *Letters* (New York: Braziller, 1962) pp. 231-232.

[2] See *Let Us Now Praise Famous Men* (Boston: Houghton Mifflin Company, 1960), and especially pp. 239-242.

[3] *The Collected Short Prose of James Agee* (Boston: Houghton Mifflin Company, 1968) p. 137.

[4] *Famous Men*, p. 13.

[5] Let us now praise famous men: notes, autograph manuscript notebook, n.d. (c. 1940) The University of Texas Library. This, and other unpublished material used in this essay, is gratefully used with the permission of the James Agee Trust.

[6] *Agee on Film*, Volume I (New York: Grosset and Dunlap, 1967) p. 405. This article originally appeared in the *Partisan Review*.

[7] *Ibid.*, p. 203.

[8] Letter "To Archie" and enclosures. Typed carbon copy manuscript, The University of Texas Library.

[9] "Popular Religion," typed carbon copy manuscript, The University of Texas Library.

[10] "Double-Take," typed carbon copy manuscript, The University of Texas Library.

[11] See "Plans for Work: October 1937," *Collected Short Prose, op. cit.*, pp. 134-135.

[12] *Letters*, p. 118.

[13] "Notes and Suggestions on the magazine under discussion," typed carbon copy manuscript, The University of Texas Library.

[14] Of course, in many ways the ideas which Agee propounded are quite similar to the interests of the Center for the Study of Popular culture. He would no doubt, have been pleased with the type and variety of studies which are regularly published in the *Journal of Popular Culture*.

II

The Tenant Book

Famous Men as Image
of a Way of Life

I

A fundamental accomplishment of Agee's *Let Us Now Praise Famous Men* is its image of tenant farming. True, the book is simultaneously the record of Agee's interaction of consciousness with the events which generated it, but it is such a record so that an accurate image of a way of life may be provided. This may appear obvious, but commentary on this complicated book is often involved either with the presence of Agee within its text, and the complexities of that technique, or with the fact that the text is ultimately a commentary about the problem of individualism.[1] Certainly *Famous Men* has immense value for these reasons. It is Agee's masterwork, and the complexity of its form is such that some even have unfortunately assumed that it is a failure.[2] Its subject matter is all individuals in an analogous situation to that of the farmers Agee lived with; and he knew as he was writing the book that his subject was constantly "expanding outward."[3] But while the importance of technique and a concern with individualism are facets of the book which should not be minimized, such concern does tend to blur the focus upon a particular culture, the core of this work.

Lear's words "Poor naked wretches . . . "[4] (III, iv, 28) constitute one of the book's epigraphs. The text is designed so that we will feel how those Agee knew felt. Those tenant farmers can easily be forgotten as Agee's elaborately devised prose is admired, or the text is used as a springboard to explain how such tenants are akin to others worldwide. The purpose of this paper is to demonstrate how an image of the impoverished lives Agee knew remains at the center of this complex book. Robert Fitzgerald correctly suggests that "between them Agee and Evans made sure that George and Annie Mae Gudger are as immortal as Priam and Hecuba, and a lot closer to home."[5] Agee's careful use of language allowed him to provide that record, yet he always reconstructed things so that the "dignity of actuality" (p. 245) is his focus.

Agee knew that his temperament and background would color the account. But such "distortion" provides as accurate an image as possible given the conditions chosen. The result is a book which resembles a lyric poem in method because of the writer's presence. That "lyric" stresses the impoverishment (of body and spirit) Agee saw in the lives of the Gudger family, and other individuals who seem to be hardly in control of their lives. The choice of material for inclusion in *Famous Men* signifies what Agee considered to be the most important elements in the formation of these particular middle Alabama lives. The result is an image of a way of life.

Famous Men is primarily a record of persons who are both materially and spiritually impoverished; yet, ironically, because they are shrunken of potentiality, there remains a dignity about their lives, the result of an intricate conjunction of land and living. Despite abuse by a system which treats them little better than animals, a beauty is beheld in the nuances of their existence. Technically, Agee's problem was how best to "contrive techniques" which would show the beauty, but also the complexity of that actuality. Ultimately, he realized, all things observed (or which are existent) are important in a consideration of such complexity, for each person is formed of a concatenation of events, and

> that which we receive yet do not recognize, nor hold in the moment's focus, is nevertheless and continuously and strengthfully planted upon our brains, upon our blood: [and] cuts its little mark: each blown leaf of a woodland a quarter-mile distant while I am absorbed in some close exactitude: each . . . registers . . . by multitudes [and] by iteration. . . . (pp. 105-106)

To account for such multitudes as they impinge upon each other is impossible. Such an accounting would require an infinite text written and read "as if all in one sentence" (p. 106). Since this could not be, the "dissonant prologue" of this text results. Its method is a series of interrelated techniques which combine a careful attention to fact with an apologetic tone which suggests that no matter how elaborate the technique, it will not suffice. Each attempt to describe or evoke is a sketch and a new beginning, and Agee does not attempt explanations or suggest solutions. He is interested merely in the "cruel radiance" of what is.

The result is a picture of lives which are heavily dependent upon the land, and of a culture caught between the agrarian and the industrial. These inhabitants of rural Alabama are locked into an existence of degradation. The fact that Agee's visit came during the most intense part of the Depression serves to emphasize the bleakness of this way of life. But his text is considerably more than a "documentary" about living conditions during the great Depression.

The book had its inception in an assignment for *Fortune* magazine. Agee was to write an article about an "average white family of tenant farmers." That rather typical documentary assignment expanded into something much more complicated. It became an attack on many of the documentaries which had preceded it, and included the personal suffering of Agee. Several parts of the book seem only about him and it is necessary to understand why he incorporated passages which concentrate on his solitary mood.[6] Finally such passages imply a clarity of understanding about the entire experience of living with these particular families. These passages are often set in late night when clarity seemed more certain than during the activities of day. The peacefulness of such remembered moments is suggestive of what was felt about facts of the whole experience. As the sleeping Gudger family is remembered, Agee recalls his felt mood in "On the Porch":

> . . . human silence obtained, prevailed, only locally, shallowly, and with the childlike and frugal dignity of a coaloil lamp stood out on a wide night meadow and of a star sustained, unraveling in one rivery sigh its irremediable vitality, on the alien size of space. (p. 20)

This fragile local quietness is (and was) a reminder of the precariousness of these men's existence, and of their intricate realtionship to the universe as well. In other similarly meditative sections, Agee develops his fascination with the quietness which surrounds the Gudgers' frail house, their only protection: a "shell and carapace, more frail against heaven than fragilest membrane of glass" (p. 53). The language suggests the kind and placement of the house, but also suggests Agee's state of mind during the particular recalled moment. At that time he was one with his surroundings. It was as if all incidental things of the world were unnoticed. That feeling of peacefulness was

> like that brief paralysis which enchants a city while wreaths are laid to a cenotaph, and, muted, a bugle's inscription shines, in the tightening just before the relaxation of this swarmed, still, silence, till, hats-on, gears grow and smooth, the lifted foot arrested in the stopshot completes its step. Once more the white mane of the dray horse flurs in the sunny air: now vibrates all that vast stone hive: into resumption, reassumption of casual living. (p. 52)

Such quiet made it seem that action had been frozen, and that the everyday busy-ness of the world was halted. Agee has in mind a still shot used in conjunction with a motion picture, and it is through his careful description of that imagined photograph that he suggests the enchantment of his felt mood. His experience of that evening (and by analogy of many similar events) had been clear, and he wanted "at all leisure" to recall the details. It was as if a brilliant ray of light illumined those moments. In his reference to the sound of a bugle, the moment's clarity is united with Agee's use of language throughout the book. The recalled moment had been as if chiseled on a monument, yet it was as fleeting as the notes of a bugle at a ceremony when the body of the person remembered is elsewhere. Such absence of immediacy is often lamented throughout the text. The inclusion of such a uniquely personal feeling of oneness with the night and natural surroundings suggests how clearly Agee, at a particular moment, sensed the interaction of his consciousness with its surroundings. The implication is that these farmers must often (perhaps unconsciously) experience the same sense of tranquility, for they are part of a whole, blended into and partaking of it in a way that Agee knows he, as "spy" and "intruder," cannot. Their lives, more fragile than their delicate houses, make a mark within surroundings which emphasize their smallness and loneliness. And such lives are part of a unity of land and living that Agee cannot ever hope to feel completely, certainly not to articulate.[7] He can provide glimpses of it through his remembered feelings.

II

But Agee knew he had to avoid writing about himself. And usually he describes how he participated in an event or observed a fact as a means of reflecting the culture. Then, facts, such as his encounter of a young couple as he seeks directions, or the remembrance of how he was forced to listen to "nigger music" against his wishes become ways of mirroring the complexity of what he saw. He maintained that no matter what he did technically, the result could only be a dim reflection of the experience. "A piece of the body torn out by the roots might be more to the point" (p. 13), he lamented, as he explained that if he could do it, the book would not be "written" at all.

This is not the place to provide an elaborate explanation of the techniques devised for the book.[8] But, ultimately, to understand what is accomplished, a reader must appreciate the complexity of the text's organization. Agee had distinct "planes" or techniques in mind as he wrote, and it can be demonstrated that distinct parts of the book are written with particular realities in mind. Thus, "On the Porch" (recall-reception) begins "*in medias res*"; but in its middle section, halfway through the book, an elaborate discussion of the problems foreseen in presenting even a fragment of this experience (problems of recording) is included.

The text is divided into many sections. Its opening pages recount chance encounters and provide glimpses of the culture. Other early parts suggest Agee's condition of mind as experienced during the visit, or modified by its remembrance. The main middle section of the book deals with carefully selected facts about the tenants' lives. Chapters entitled "Money," "Shelter," "Clothing," "Education," and "Work" isolate aspects of the culture. Each of those technically different sections is designed to show how the lives of these sharecroppers are intertwined with the land. Especially in this middle section an image of a way of life is provided.

The dominance of natural forces is central to this vision of a way of life. For this is a culture which draws its sustenance from the land, as does the cotton for which the family appears to exist. These are used lives. Cotton is raised within a system which traps its producers in a cycle of reiterative labor.[9] It becomes the main thread in an elaborate network which contributes to their impoverishment. But paradoxically it is the land also that allows these persons to live at all. These tenants are degraded, not so much because of their isolation from society, but ironically because of their contact with it, and what they are is a reflection of their relationship to society and to the land. In "On the Porch" Agee describes his awareness of a creek and of all of the fields and streams and rivers throughout the countryside connected together and flowing toward the Mississippi as part of an intricate network which drains life away from the land. These tenant lives are part of the same intricacy. The river system is like a vine, but a vine which "takes growth not by the radiant outward energy which compels a branched tree to burst still further into branches but always by a sinking away of its energy toward the center, as leaves are drawn into the wake of an auto" (p. 251). This passage concludes with a description of the Mississippi at New Orleans as a rectal discharge. The implication is clear. Because of the system the profit from the labor of these people is not returned to them, but sucked into the wake of a technological society. Agee's awareness of abuse and degradation is further delineated in his chapter entitled "Work," one of the most elaborate and imaginative descriptions of planting and picking cotton ever written.

The land dominates. And the fields are merely "workrooms," extensions of houses which seem like feeble near-childlike structures. Because of the land these people are able to live, yet because of it they struggle. And their struggle is immensely difficult precisely because of the paradoxical profusion of nature. Thus working all day usually provides only enough of a return on one's investment to maintain the position attained by yesterday's work. It is like an enormous treadmill, the parts of which are wearing out. Cutting a wagonload of firewood and going into town for its sale may result not in profit, but perhaps in letting the load go for a nickel, so that the wood will not have to be brought all the way back home. It would be better if there were not so much wood or cotton.

To live as these families do—dependent upon nature, but also horribly dependent upon a system—places them in a nearly impossible situation. They would, Agee implies, like so much to have what they imagine others have. Even in a small matter such as cigarettes Agee is aware of the tensions felt by a man like George Gudger. When he first met Gudger, he offered him a cigarette. Later he realized that George

likes machine-made cigarettes less well than those he rolls
for himself, but he is fond of the meaning and distinction
which is in their price, and would probably always use
them if he could afford them. (pp. 399-400)

The major middle section of the book, a series of chapters
subtitled "Some Findings and Comments," begins with one called
"Money." Appropriately this is a succinct account which begins with
the ironic words of F. D. R.: "You are farmers; I am a farmer myself."
A brief harsh statement of fact suffices to suggest the scarcity of money
which exists.

The section immediately following stands, in elaborate contrast, as an attempt to show what was perceived through Agee's
observation of a typical shelter. Here the forty-second Psalm ("I will go
unto the altar of God," the prayer at the foot of the altar before Mass)
establishes a tone. These houses are symbols, and Agee, as the receiver
of these "sacraments," emphasizes that it is with the same reverence as
at a religious service that one must approach them. His inspection of
the Gudger house and its contents was done with the same respect, he
says, as a priest touching the "blessed cloths" (p. 188). Agee appends
a two-page outline and notes to indicate what he is attempting in this
ninety-page section. It is his single most elaborate attempt to present
aspects of this rural culture.

The houses lived in were of the frailest variety, but they remain
"poetry." The Gudgers' house stood "at the end of a mile of dwindled
branch road" as if civilization dribbled away before it reached such a
peculiar structure. It resembled "a museum model or an establishment
for large dolls" (p. 127). Such houses, surrounded by the "workrooms,"
seem almost swallowed by natural forces and a "roof of uncontrollable
chance" (p. 129). But these houses share the characteristics of more
sophisticated dwellings, while they remain "rudimentary as a child's
drawing,"and bare, clean, and sober as "only Doric architecture . . .
can hope to approach" (p. 144). It is as if simple wooden fabrics were
stitched into only a crude approximation of a garment. (The metaphor
is Agee's.) In their making, the wood, with its grain still visible, is
crucified into an approximation and imitation of more elaborate and
"civilized" structures.

Like the lives of those who inhabit them, these houses are
formed of the interaction of "nature and science." The wall boards,
with grain and knots "such as Beethoven's deafness compelled," are

"sawn and stripped across into rigid ribbons and by rigid lines and boundaries . . . yet not in perfect line (such is the tortured yet again perfect innocence of men, caught between the pulls of nature and science)" (pp. 145-146). Such structures honestly express the lives which they shelter. But how can their beauty be suggested? One image of the delicate and powerful grandeur of the Gudgers' home compares it to

> the effort of one man to hold together upon one instrument, as if he were breaking a wild monster to bridle and riding, one of the larger fugues of Bach, on an organ, as against the slick collaborations and effortless climaxes of the same piece in the manipulations of an orchestra. (p. 144)

Here the prose rhythm assists to suggest how this building is sustained. The house, while awkwardly nailed together, seems united as if by the power of a primitive artist. In the concluding phrases the manipulative quality of other more sophisticated procedures is suggested by the heavy incorporation of Latinate words and halting rhythm. The complexity of this prose is indicative of Agee's realization of the difficulty of what he was attempting to suggest. His realization that such a house seems held together by the extraordinary efforts of a single person provides an insight into the complexity of a seemingly simple house and of a seemingly simple culture and when one begins to understand the complexity of such a structure, a symbol for a way of life, then the complexity of that way of life is glimpsed.

Even the odor of the Gudgers' eight-year-old house is noted. If properly observed and presented, Agee knew, such information would allow a reader to come closer to an understanding of how people live. Yet this odor is of a complexity that challenges words because it is a combination "classical in every thoroughly poor white Southern country house" (p. 154). Part of that complexity is achieved with elaborate listings, such as the following:

> Of sleep, of bedding, and of breathing. . . . Odors of staleness from clothes hung away . . . the odor of corn: in sweat, or on the teeth, and breath. . . . All these so combined into one that they are all and always present in balance. (pp. 154-155)

All the objects in the Gudgers' house combine to reveal facets of their lives. The furniture in the front bedroom is positioned with extreme symmetricality. Several of Agee's paragraphs begin: "Exactly . . ." and as he outlines how the stark furniture is arranged, one perceives that the furniture is sad and dismal, and that the symmetrical arrangement is an almost vain attempt to give the room some dignity. Yet that attempt does succeed. By such attention to the commonplace Agee shows his reader facets of a way of living.

Similarly the objects of the Gudgers' house "in the standing and spacings of mute furnishings" (p. 134) possess "a beauty and wonder greater than any music ever made" (p. 139). If perceived properly those objects reveal fantastic amounts of information about their owners. Photographs and old calendars and magazine covers and labels from cans are displayed on the Gudgers' wall. Baby dresses are carefully laid in drawers. All manner of junk, worn-out clothes, and used-up furniture stand as mute commentary. Several lists of objects which are the result of "almost endless saving" (p. 133) are provided throughout this section. Thus, Agee takes note of a broom:

> the cheap thirty-to-forty-cent kind and . . . nearly new, but do not be misled: the old one, still held in limbo because nothing is thrown away, was well used before it was discarded: It has about the sweeping power of a club foot. (p. 180)

For this is a culture unable to make things. Except for the crude corn-shuck hats made by the Ricketts family and one hierloom, the book contains no mention of handcrafted objects made by these people. For they do not possess the skill, nor time to make, and they have no money to buy. The result is a makeshift existence with only the fragments of an older more independent folk-culture constantly impinged upon by the newer industrial-technological one. Agee knows that much of what he observes would go absolutely unnoticed by tenants. (The women are certainly not aware that their dresses are imitations of imitations of imitations.)

The shelter section ends with a "recessional"—a lyrical and factual account of animals and plants and insects, for such creatures surround the house, and contribute to its essence and way of life. The recessional is "merely another suggestion of what is textured within any one of these silent and simple appearing horizons and of what in and around even one of these blank wood houses is sown into these human lives" (p. 218). The recessional again suggests the natural texture of these holy lives.

A similar, but more severely restrained technical procedure is used in the chapter which follows about clothing. Here the starkest details are arranged to contrive an effect. A few phrases about George Gudger on Sunday morning suggest how awkward he feels in the formality of Sunday dress: "the hat is still only timidly dented into shape. . . . The crease is still sharp in the trousers" (p. 257). As an indication of the care taken in this section one need only know that Agee devotes pages to the feel and texture and variations of color of a pair of overalls, clothes which resemble a harness for a "used animal." His attention to the overalls is a further way of suggesting an aspect of these lives. The beauty of common workclothes stands in contrast to the awkwardness of store-purchased clothes. Details about the mutations of cloth of common workclothes provide insight when what is ordinarily considered unimportant is observed carefully.

For the accounts about both shelter and clothing the report of fact is predominant. Still other parts of the text provide an image of cotton tenantry by relying upon what Agee was told by others, yet embellished by his imagination. Such are the chapters "Education" and "Work." Work is the heart of this way of life. The structure of the book is such that it is apparent that everything about these lives is built around their constant "work." Thus this subject provides the last major part of "findings." It begins with the characteristic apology by Agee about his inadequacy to suggest the depths of his subject. He cannot provide "the image it should be," but he will let his attempt "stand as the image it is" (p. 319). "It is for clothing, and for food, and for the shelter, by these to sustain their lives, that they work" (p. 319). In this section the work cycle of each year is evoked, and the reiterative quality of the work described: "the same set of leverages" year after year and year.

Cotton is the main crop, and raising it the function of these lives, a job "by which one stays alive and in which one's life is made a cheated ruin" (p. 326). Agee's indirect knowledge of cotton farming, combined with his imagination, provides insight into how it must feel to perform such drudgery. Remarks made to him (or overheard) are fitted into his account. After the preparation of the land and the planting of the cotton have been minutely described, paragraphs are devoted to a consideration of the lull before picking. This is one of the worst times for the farmer, a "terrible leisure," as "the year's fate is being quietly fought out between agencies over which he has no control" (p. 334). Then the cotton's growth is described. Then the picking itself. Then he imagines how the fields would look, and how particular persons might work in the fields. Agee suggests how it must feel to work in a field by a blending of distilled fact with metaphor. He sees the field as a "white maturing oven [with] the enlarged bolls . . . "; then continues in the concrete, "a rusty green, then bronze . . . split and splayed open . . ." but quickly his imagination qualifies with the phrase: "each in a loose vomit of cotton" (p. 336). Like most of the section headed "Picking Season," this phrase is written as a "continuum" based on facts, but constructed from imagination. The vision is Agee's but it is meant to suggest what the farmers behold.

After the long-awaited first bale is ginned, the family returns to its home:

> It is as if those who were drawn in full by the sun and their own effort and sucked dry at a metal heart were restored, were sown once more at large upon the slow breaths of their country, in the precisions of some mechanic and superhuman hand. (p. 341)

The implication is that these people are part of a natural, yet somehow also unnatural, cycle.

III

Agee constantly assures his reader that it is impossible to know a way of life, or evoke it with a verbal approximation. With that resigned attitude, he arranged his text so that the final major portion of text is entitled "Inductions." After some three hundred and fifty pages of preparation Agee feels his reader should be ready to draw some conclusions by himself. There we go back with him to first meetings with the families and receive an account of those early comments "as they happened." Particularities described take on universal meanings, and for this reason Agee knew that what he chose to describe, if described carefully, would provide an insight into a culture.

There is no "average white tenant family." But Agee's love for these persons, and his rage at their degradation, drove him to sketch the "dignity of [their] actuality." The resulting text does provide a picture of a way of life.

Notes

[1] Peter Ohlin's critical study *Agee* (New York: Obolensky, 1966) approaches the text, in Agee's words, as "'an effort in human actuality.'" and is primarily concerned with the language as an elaborate verbal gesture in which both reader and writer participate. In his critical pamphlet, Erling Larsen comments on the book as "both a piece of reportage and an agonizing self-examination" ([Minneapolis: University of Minnesota Press, 1971], p. 26). Commentary which moves away from an emphasis on technique includes Alan Holder's article "Encounter in Alabama," *Virginia Quarterly Review*, 42 (Spring 1966), 189, which demonstrates how Agee depoliticizes his subject, but at the same time ultimately finds the subject in the cosmos itself. A related extensive treatment of Agee's writing is J. Douglas Perry, Jr.'s dissertation "James Agee and the American Romantic Tradition" (Temple University, 1968) in which elements of *Famous Men* are related to American Romanticism.

[2] See pp. 41-58 of Kenneth Seib's *James Agee: Promise and Fulfillment* (Pittsburgh: University of Pittsburgh Press, 1968).

[3] *The Letters of James Agee to Father Flye*, edited by James H. Flye (New York: George Braziller, Inc., 1962), p. 104.

[4] *Let Us Now Praise Famous Men* (Boston: Houghton Mifflin Company, 1960), p. xviii. All subsequent references are to this edition.

[5] Robert Fitzgerald, "A Memoir," in *the Collected Short Prose of James Agee* (Boston: Houghton Mifflin Company, 1969), p. 49.

[6] Initial reaction to *Famous Men* implied Agee was too much present within the text. Reviews and much subsequent commentary follow the pattern of a typical early review by John C. Cort (*The Commonweal*, September 12, 1941, p. 499): He suggests the text "is too repetitious, too obscure, particularly too obsessed with the author's complex reactions to his subject and to everything else from Cezanne to Kafka to his own relatives." Seib mistakenly asserts that "the book, like an oversized suit, hangs loose in several places" (p. 55).

[7] Compare Ohlin's argument: "the *only* way to see Agee's work is not as a book about 'sharecropping' but as a book about the writing of a book about 'sharecropping'" (p. 106, Ohlin's italics). Such emphasis does not give sufficient attention to Agee's concern with this way of life.

[8] The technical procedure developed treats four different kinds of reality. Each reality necessitates a different "plane of writing." The first of these centers around the fact that he wrote of what he uniquely experienced. It is a contemplative mode of writing and the quietness of "On the Porch" is of this reality. The second reality recollects experience, "'as it happened': the straight narrative at the prow as from the first . . . it cut unknown water." This "plane" focuses upon particular events "as they occurred." The third reality, "recall and memory from the present," is the most important method developed for the delineation of the culture itself. On this level factual reporting is essential, but also the imagination is used to give clarity to the remembrance of facts about these people. The fourth reality is the technical problem of recording: "an organic part of the experience" (p. 243). Each of these approaches is not wholly distinct from the others in the finished text; often the simultaneity of their existence is as important as their distinctness. The result of Agee's struggle to be honest with his material is an elaborate rhetorical strategy which draws the reader into the book.

[9] A partial carbon copy manuscript of *Famous Men*, in the possession of the Library of the University of Texas, includes an unused manuscript version of the chapter "Work," from which only "selections" were taken for the book. There Agee elaborately emphasizes the reiterative quality of all physical labor. See my edition of this unpublished manuscript, "The Complete 'Work' Chapter for James Agee's *Let Us Now Praise Famous Men*," Volume 15 of *The Texas Quarterly*.

The Writer's Consciousness of Technique

Let Us Now Praise Famous Men (1941) is a text that resulted from the happy conjunction of James Agee's vast ambition and the specific needs that he saw generated during the 1930s. Looking at the contemporary scene, he could see beyond what many artists saw, and therefore *Famous Men* became a text that goes far beyond the use of particular facts to document observations or support a thesis. This is a text that evokes and honors reality, not uses it.

Agee knew that to contrive a fully adequate technique would be impossible, and he sensed this before he began to write; but five years of energy went into the intricate composition of this, his most problematic book, and the resultant text is, on one level, a record of a struggle with a project about which he could not stop feeling strong emotion. On another level the text gives us one of the most complete pictures of the 1930s, and this seems to be so because manifold purposes support the composition of Agee's ambitious experiment. Its charged rhetoric provides enormous amounts of information both about him and about its ostensible subject matter, tenant farming.

Agee warned readers that this text was an inquiry into "the predicaments of human divinity," while he also stressed that his effort was an attempt to "recognize the stature of a portion of unimagined existence, and to contrive techniques proper to its recording, communication, analysis, and defense."[1] In a notebook, written as the book was composed, he sketched his subject matter and insisted that at the "centre" of the work the following was to be found: "[1] At the centre, every recapturable instant of those eight weeks spent in the middle South; [2] At the centre again: ourselves, and our instruments (both camera and language). The primary instrument is individual human consciousness; [3] Again at the centre: these three families chosen with such pain to 'represent' their kind."[2]

Such a complexity of intention and determination to provide

means of access to so many facts of a particular experience illuminates both the success and "failure" of Agee's unusual text. He knew that he could not achieve a unity that some writers might desire, nor one that most readers would look for. In his preamble he stated: "No doubt I shall worry myself that I am taking too long getting started, and shall seriously distress myself over my inability to create an organic, mutually sustaining and dependent, and as it were musical form: but I must remind myself that I started with the first world I wrote, and that the centers of my subject are shifty" (p. 10). Above all, he was concerned with recording the sacramental reality of particular lives, and experiences, yet as he reconstructed such facts he knew they expanded outward. He had been thinking about related technical problems for years before this *Fortune* magazine assignment to go to the South.[3] The Alabama assignment provided him with an impetus to develop methods that might begin to catch the rhythm and complexity of the *un*imagined. Agee knew if such stylistic contrivance was to be effective, the technique would have to be severely controlled. (Ultimately he even admitted that the specific trip to Alabama—and the ostensible subject matter—was not of particular significance to him. Most important was this attempt to develop ways of reflecting the dignity of an *un*imagined world.)

Because Agee attempted so many different things within this text, he accomplished various things. The text has been carefully studied in relation to the development of American romanticism. It has been interpreted as the key to Agee's maturation of artistic capability. It has been described as a book about the writing of a book about tenant farming.[4] And each of these approaches is correct. The present essay is an analytical consideration of some of the technical devices "contrived" to evoke the reality of what was observed, remembered, and imagined because of a few weeks' trip to Alabama in 1936. Agee's text has been called a failure.[5] This analysis seeks to clarify the complexity of his method, and to show how it grew out of the particular historical situation of the mid-1930s, a time when Agee was learning to look carefully at the "dignity of actuality" that was part of his contemporary America. But Agee was interested in revealing, not in suggesting solutions. This fact sets his text off from related works.

One of the reasons this text has been so often misunderstood could be that it seems to be composed of so many different components. Agee was aware of its diversity (even incongruity) but he felt if he was going to convey the complexity of his subject, and in a manner appropriate to his vision, his mode of communication would have to be complex. In his preamble he says: "And if there are questions in my mind how to undertake this communication, and there are many, I must let the least of them be, whether I am boring you, or whether I am taking too long getting started, and too clumsily. If I bore you, that is that. If I am clumsy, that may indicate partly the difficulty of my subject, and the seriousness with which I am trying to take what hold I can of it" (p. 10). His subject was the mundane daily life of farmers in middle Alabama. He wanted to retell his experience with them in as truthful a way as possible "without either dissection into science, or digestion into art, but with the whole of consciousness" (p. 11). That he knew it was impossible to accomplish such a task is reflected in the many apologetic statements sprinkled throughout the book.

Writing in the thirties when it was sometimes easiest to think as a member of a group, Agee believed he had first to communicate the fact that he wrote of separate, distinct human beings as apprehended within a unique texture of events. Each person was "a human being, not like any other human being so much as he is like himself" (p. 232). Because each person was respected as distinct and holy, the dignity of the human person serves as the basic recurring motif, providing a dimension of religious awe and celebration through which this dignity is presented.

Language and, even more, obvious external use of religious forms, strengthen this religious motif. Because each person is distinct and therefore to be respected, Agee felt that one of his duties as writer was to suggest how that individuality was brought about. Influences of varying sizes and shapes come into contact with particular individuals, and with each contact some change is made in the person. "It would be our business," Agee wrote, "to show how through every instant of every day of every year of his existence alive he is from all sides streamed inward upon, bombarded, pierced, destroyed by that enormous sleeting of all objects forms and ghosts how great how small no matter, which surround and whom his senses take: in as great and perfect and exact particularity as we can name them" (p. 110).

But while trying to adhere to particularities, he also knew that he had been affected by what he had seen. His perception had acted as contributor to the effect. Agee's aesthetic therefore focuses attention on details remembered but always as remembered (perhaps changed and distorted) by him. Such a method would almost surely insure disfavor among some readers and critics of leftist political persuasions. Agee's consciousness remains central.

That the recorder, Agee himself, was in many ways a poor instrument for the recording of what he relates is considered of prime importance. To judge better about incidents and objects included within the text, Agee felt that the reader had to be given adequate knowledge of the writer. One extreme example of this conviction is the inclusion, under the caption "Intermission: Conversation in the Lobby," of Agee's impulsive answers to a series of questions asked of American writers by the *Partisan Review*: questions, for instance, about the duties of the writer in the late 1930s, should war develop, seemed an impertinence to Agee, who flippantly answered he had always considered himself to be at war. He wanted his readers to know some of his biases; they might more easily then draw conclusions about other parts of the book. Similarly, this text is replete with remembrances of Agee's childhood and experiences only obliquely related to the tenant material.

But Agee's presence within the text is not only to provide the reader with knowledge of the limitations of the recording instrument but also to indicate that what had happened to him was unique, consequently important, and therefore to be part of an accurately recorded experience. Several explicit statements are made concerning problems that arose in the recording of the experience. Such technical problems were, to Agee's mind, integrated with the whole experience. The actual event, its remembrance, and the problem of how to combine the best of each of these confronted him. He knew that what he hoped finally to accomplish was really beyond the capabilities of language, but at the same time he knew that language possessed distinct qualities separate from other modes of communication and for which it could and should be valued. He stressed that "words could, I believe, be made to do or to tell anything within human conceit. That is more than can be said of the instruments of any other art. . . . It may, however, be added: words like all else are limited by certain laws. To call their achievement crippled in relation to what they have tried to convey may be all very well: but to call them crippled in their completely healthful obedience to their own nature is again a mistake: the same mistake as the accusation of a cow for her unhorsiness" (pp. 236-237).

His doubts about achieving all he desired are reflected throughout his text; primarily these are doubts about how best to handle the technical problems. From the very beginning of the book the writer's attention is divided between the problems that faced him as he tried to write of what had happened and his doubts about his very right to be prying into the lives he writes about: in other words, moral problems. Also in this way Agee's text is a step beyond so many "documentaries" of the 1930s.[6] He labors the point that possibly what he is doing should not be done at all. He opens the book proper by saying, "It seems to me curious, not to say obscene and thoroughly terrifying, that it could occur to an association of human beings drawn together thorough need and chance and for profit into a company, an organ of journalism, to pry intimately into the lives of an undefended and appallingly damaged group of human beings" (p. 7). At one point he says if it were possible there would be "no writing at all" (p. 13). Yet remembering that Beethoven once said "he who understands my music can never know unhappiness again," Agee writes he must say the same of his perception. If he could have communicated all that he felt he knew that his moral problems, the doubts about his right to attempt such a book, would be eliminated. Agee's qualification is that "performance is another matter" (p. 16). The fact that he was so aware of such problems is what ultimately makes his text a success. Knowing that he must ultimately fail, he took on the challenge of suggesting what he sensed and wanted to communicate.

The material for *Famous Men* was gathered by living with one family, the Gudgers, for a period of about one month, but close ties were also developed with two other families. It was hoped that in this way a representative idea could be gained about tenant farming in general. Upon these ideas he elaborated and developed broad statements that concerned all tenant farmers. The best example of this type of elaboration is the section entitled "Work," wherein Agee blends his love of those with whom he had lived with a realization that millions are forced to lead lives much like those of the Gudgers, the Woods, and the Ricketts. These three particular families therefore served as a base from which imagination flowed toward all tenant-farm families throughout the South.

The text of the book as a whole finally concerns itself not just with sharecroppers, or even with workers in the United States, but with all who live in the world.[7] In 1938, as he was working on this manuscript, Agee wrote Father James Harold Flye to explain how he was faced with the problem of his whole subject matter "intensifying" itself. "The whole problem and nature of existence"[8] was present within his questioning mind. Thus while the text is a picture of Agee's unique remembrance as he devises procedures appropriate for this retelling, it is as well a commentary about the fragility of man's existence. Many of the more meditative parts of the book suggest no writer more than Thoreau. Thus moving from the particulars of living in Alabama, and framed by his dissatisfaction with much that had been called "documentary," Agee wrote a text that is precise and that radiates outward beyond the particularities of its inspiration.

Famous Men functions like a poem, even though its author clearly urges throughout that a work of "Art" was not intended. Agee had to write of his experience, and because he was so inextricably involved with those about whom he wrote, his basic manner of presentation was lyrical. Intense personal emotion was at the core, even when he wrote about a very plain "object" or "atmosphere." For such "objects and atmospheres have a sufficient intrinsic beauty and stature that it might be well if the describer became more rather than less shameless: if objects and atmospheres for the secret sake of which it is customary to write a story or poem, and which are chronically relegated to a menial level of decoration or at best illumination, were handled and presented on their own merits without either distortion or apology. Since when has a landscape painter apologized for painting landscapes?" (p. 239). It is significant that he notes immediately following this passage that Cocteau had remarked of Picasso that "the subject matter is merely the excuse for the painting, and that Picasso does away with the excuse" (p. 239). Such a comment is an indirect admission by Agee of how important his presence is within the text. That presence is important even when he presents a record of something for its own sake, as when he records all the contents of a particular drawer in the Gudgers' bedroom.

Agee wants his reader to feel as if he too were in a living situation. In the preamble he had suggested that the text might be read aloud; and he indicated that he was striving for a new literary form that would be analogous to music. Ultimately, the form he developed was one that relied upon several basic techniques that flow into one another.

Because of the complexity of the variegated experience that

had been undergone, Agee felt that several different techniques would have to be employed to communicate his experience verbally. The point of view with which he approached his writing is reflected in the following passage:

> The whole job may well seem messy to you. But part of my point is that experience offers itself in richness and variety and in many more terms than one and that it may therefore be wise to record it no less variously. Much of the time I shall want to tell of particulars very simply, in their own terms: but from any set of particulars it is possible and perhaps useful to generalize. In any case I am the sort of person who generalizes: and if for your own convenience and mine I left that out, I would be faking and artifacting right from the start. (pp. 244-245)

Each technique he employed represents an attempt to communicate an absolute "realness," yet the subject matter differs in three basic ways: the first of Agee's "realities" centers around the simple fact that he wrote about what *he* had experienced. What exactly his reaction was, later described within the text, becomes a basic item to be communicated. Second, he wrote about real persons and events. He did not go to Alabama and gather materials for a composite picture of tenant farmers, using bits of many lives and his imagination to fit together a work of "Art." However, there are millions who must face essentially the same problems as those Agee knew, and therefore he had to communicate a third type of reality. To help his reader understand how widespread were the conditions described, he was forced to generalize. Therefore from the particular things that he saw and recorded, his concern and love extended to millions of other humans leading lives similar to those that he knew and described.

Agee himself, in the section "On the Porch" (a part of the book that was written early), spoke of handling the technical problems of recording what he had seen and felt "from four planes." It is possible to demonstrate how each of the sections of *Famous Men* is built on a distinct level.

A study of Agee's concept of planes of writing yields insights into the complexity of *Famous Men*, and, indeed, whole sections can be profitably identified as being consciously crafted with particular planes in mind. But still other methods reflect Agee's consciousness of technique and demonstrate how he moved from the particulars observed to the implications beyond. Both his construction of a "continuum" and his precise use of stylized language emphasizes his reverence for the subject matter. Such techniques also emphasize Agee's vision.

In his development of the continuum the controlled fusion of elements already mentioned takes place. Thus, as Agee writes in a continuum the many "centres" he mentions in his notebook entry begin to move closer together and, by implication, he condemns the easy observations of others. Agee is concerned with the point of view expressed in the following words:

> George Gudger is a man et cetera. But obviously in the effort to tell of him (by example) as truthfully as I can, I am limited. I know him only so far as I know him, and only in those terms in which I know him; and all of that depends as fully on who I am as on who he is.
>
> I am confident of being able to get at a certain form of the truth about him, *only if* I am as faithful as possible to Gudger as I know him, to Gudger as, in his actual flesh and life (but there again always in my mind's and memory's eye) he is . . . I would do just as badly to simplify or eliminate myself from this picture as to simplify or invent character, places or atmospheres. A chain of truths did actually weave itself and run through: it is their texture that I want to represent, not betray, nor pretty up into art. (pp. 239-240)

We remember that for him the camera was the "central instrument of our time," and Agee's immense respect for the camera has its basis in the fact that it is "incapable of recording anything but absolute dry truth" (pp. 11,234). With this in mind he admits as he "catalogues" what he saw that a camera might do a better job. Yet language, he believed, has merits distinctly its own. With language as his basic instrument, used as a photographer might use a camera but fused with the poetic imagination, a writer is able to give a sense of an experience as seen with eye *and* mind (both at a particular time and as recalled later as well). For Agee such a fusion can best be presented as a continuum.

A continuum is therefore an extremely successful fusion of many methods employed throughout the text. Indeed, when considered in relationship to Agee's planes, it is evident that this device cannot be separated from his second category, "as it happened," yet it includes regular use of plane three, recall *and* imagination. Looking at specific pages headed "The room beneath the house," we see Agee's attempt to fuse straight description with mental reactions both initially and later. These pages consist of six paragraphs and a prose poem (pp. 147-149). Here an instant of *un*imagined reality is recaptured; but the writer simultaneously reveals himself and places an imagined family in focus through a kind of extended meditation. It is Agee's success in fusing all of these things in his meditation that sets *Let Us Now Praise Famous Men* off as a superior achievement.

The first paragraph is descriptive: "The rear edges of the house rest in part on stacked stones, in part on the dirt . . . forward edges . . . on thick rounded sections of logs." Here the writer attempts to give an accurate description. But the second paagraph shows an immediate shift to metaphor. The dirt beneath the house, a "cold plaque," is compared to a wall against which "a picture has been hung for years." Agee wonders to what other uses this land could have been put. Only by chance is it a home site; it could have been as easily "field, pasture, forest." The second paragraph then is imaginative: yet it is connected closely with the "reality" of a particular instant recalled which brought about the imagined extension.

A step further is taken in the third unit. Here Agee imagines how this house was built: "lumber of other land was brought rattling in yellow wagonloads and caught up between hammers." A house was built to "hold this shape of earth denatured; yet in whose history this house shall have passed soft and casually as a snowflake fallen on black spring ground, which thaws in touching." The construction and decay of all houses is suggested by these sentences, which reveal how the perceiver's mind works. Agee has used what he saw as a means to extend his awareness and to meditate about all men.

The fourth paragraph returns to the immediate scene, and in this long unit there is constant movement from the concrete to the abstract, or from what was almost "verbally photographed" to what was imagined. Here it becomes a matter of Agee's imagining how children of a particular family might act. He says, "There in the chilly and small dust . . . the subtle funnels of doodlebugs whose teasing, of a broomstraw, is one of the patient absorptions of kneeling childhood." The thought of the children is a personal reaction, yet part of the total experience as recalled. Inclusion of such mental reactions helps the reader to see as Agee did. Objects are described in their physical terms; for example: "an emptied and flattened twenty-gauge shotgun shell, its metal green, lettering still visible." But other objects lend themselves well to more imaginative description. For instance, Agee writes that a string of ants "a long and slender infinitesimally rustling creek and system of ants in their traffic."

The "clean pine underside" of the house looked new to Agee, and this "fresh and bridal" appearance sets the stage for the fifth unit of this short section, the prose-poem. This poem, only a few lines in length, is a meditation about how quickly the expectations of those entering new homes are brought to ruin:

> (O therefore in the cleanly quiet, calm hope, secret odor, awaiting, of each new dwelling squared by men on air, he sorrowful, as of the sprung trap, the slim wrist gnawn, the little disastrous fox:
> It stands up in the sun and the bride smiles: quite soon the shelves are papered: the new forks taste in the food:
> Ruin, ruin is in our hopes: nor hope, help, any healing:)

The sight of the lumber beneath the house, woven into the total experience, set such thoughts working in Agee's mind. The poem (prayer), written after the experience, helps to clarify his actual feelings of that time but also reveals Agee's later reactions. It adds to the understanding of the writer's intentions throughout the book, one of those being to meditate about all who must lead lives similar to those of the Gudgers.

His final two paragraphs concern themselves with the house proper and its relation to the "room beneath." The house is "the flat scarce-lifted stone, the roof and firmament." This underside, "shelter and graveyard . . . and meditation space of children," is covered over by a "wide inch-thick plat of wood, swept with straws and not seldom scrubbed, soaped and spreaded with warmth of water." In this final paragraph, Agee incorporates things observed at other times—how, for instance, the floor was cleaned. Thus the meditation has become (by implication) one about all houses and all children who play in and under them. Yet above all it remains a meditation on Agee's original meditation.

Agee approached his subject matter with a devotion akin to traditional religion as it approaches the worship of God. Erik Wensberg has noted that an outline of *Famous Men* reads like the program for a

Protestant church service: "The book's design, presented in a kind of program at the front, is that of a religious service. One moves from Verses (p. 5) to Preamble (p. 7) to Inductions (p. 359)—which begins, for no explicit reason (with the Forty-second Psalm) . . . to the signification of the triumphal recessional."[9]

One goal of *Famous Men* is to stress the writer's reverence for living persons and existing things, yet Agee knew from the beginning of the writing that the "texture" of the events that had been experienced must ultimately remain inexplicable. It is, however, clear that events that are inexplicable, those that do not shed their mystery, are often "dearer"—in the words of Emerson—than events "we can see to the end of."[10] Such inexplicability, Agee's wonder at the events he witnesses, is indirectly responsible for the ultimate form of his text.

Agee's specialized uses of language are precipitated by the mystery of the events written about. One might feel that parts of the language of this text are rhetorical, in the sense of something stylistically added; but Agee's involvement is always at the core, and that involvement necessitates unusual uses of language. Kenneth Burke's observations about the ubiquity of rhetoric in human situations are of assistance in explaining why Agee relied upon such rhetorical uses of language in this text.

Agee saw particular human beings as part of a divided human community. Burke argues that division within any community gives rise to a universal communicative situation, and that therefore rhetoric as such is found in all communicative situations. The more complex a situation is, the greater is the need for rhetorical devices when that situation is communicated. Rhetoric is not merely a calculated use of language and linguistic resources. It is also a means toward achieving social cohesion. Thus, when we read any section of *Famous Men* and are moved by it, the language in that section acts rhetorically. With such rhetoric Agee makes an indirect identification between his readers and subject. (Some parts of his text were first experimentally written in very plain prose that even a child would understand. Agee abandoned that method; however, had he used it, it too would be describable as a "rhetorical" structure.)[11]

Just as there can be courtship only insofar as there is division, so also will there be a need for rhetorical structure in proportion to the division within mankind. Rhetoric, Burke writes, is the mode of appeal essential for bridging the conditions of estrangement natural to society as we know it. Thus the rhetorical element becomes most important in a section such as "Colon: Curtain Speech." In "Colon," a generalized meditation about all who live in situations similar to those of the particular tenant families whom Agee knew, rhetorical structure is relatively more important than in a deliberately antipoetic section such as the "Work" chapter.

Because a rhetorical structure, resulting from unusual language uses, is significant throughout Agee's text and is a means whereby writer indirectly appeals to reader, the question arises, To what degree may that rhetoric have been consciously planned? In one respect much of the rhetoric in *Famous Men* was not planned at all, for most of the text was *not* constructed in the manner that an orator might plan a speech in order to elicit a response from an audience. Yet as a document of Agee's responses to a particular situation, the text is intricately planned and executed. And while any desire to appeal to his readers may have been unconscious, the method of presenting the experience is a rhetorical one. Also, because Agee wanted to involve the reader as much as possible, the text was written with the possibility of its being read aloud in mind. Alliteration, metaphor, rhythm, and specialized vocabulary: all are facets of a rhetorical structure that resulted because of the writer's desire to suggest for the reader, as closely as verbally possible, the texture of experiences that he underwent. Agee's thoughts and acts were affected by interest in those about whom he wrote. Accordingly his use of language suggests an impassioned involvement with those about whom he wrote. Also because the text was written partly in disgust with a glib, more or less accepted "documentary" style that tended to oversimplify events, Agee's language contains an undercurrent of rebellion that contributes to its rhetorical appeal.

Agee was sure that most documentary writers did not become deeply enough involved (and such an accusation would apply to much of the writing that he himself had done for *Fortune* magazine). An example is relevant. If a person's pet is killed violently, the effect of the death upon that person is a fantastically complex event that ultimately cannot be adequately transformed into language. Especially the feelings of the owner are inexplicable; the death remains for him a mystery.[12]

A fundamental fact of *Famous Men* is Agee's personal involvement. Generally, the more intensely personal his insights (and accordingly the more difficult to verbalize), the more often there is a highly structured presentation. Burke suggests that often events such as those described by Agee must remain mysteries, only to be communicated by means of "incantation." Even then only a suggestion of the complexity of the felt emotions can be attained. Thus as a situation is more intensely felt, the need arises for a more comprehensive means of expressing that feeling; but unfortunately as the feeling increases the difficulty of communicating it increases also. Probably Agee did not feel as strongly about making an appeal to his readers (suggesting an identification between his reactions and the potential readers of the book, although that element is present) as he felt the need of making an identification with those about whom he wrote.

Identification in its simplest terms is a deliberate device, as used for instance by a politician. Franklin Roosevelt said, "You are farmers: I am a farmer myself." Agee ironically placed that quotation at the beginning of his "precise" about "Money," implying that identification is vastly more complicated when one is emotionally involved. Identification can be an end, "as when people earnestly yearn to identify themselves with some group or other." With such identification there is a partially idealistic motive, "somewhat compensatory to real differences or division, which the rhetoric of identification would transcend." It appears that such an idealistic motive was part of Agee's intent. In Burke's language, when one identifies himself with another, he becomes consubstantial with that person (or thing). In a written discourse a writer is faced with the problem of making the identification with another person or event clear, or at least apparent. Agee wants to suggest his identification with these farmers; yet he also (at least unconsciously) wants to set up an identification between himself and the other "intellectuals" who would read his text. For Burke, all structure as we know it, whether in speech or story, is a mode of identification. And such structure is a (possibly unconscious) appeal to the needs of a potential audience.[13] This is to say that while Agee had made a strong identification with the sharecroppers, the mystery of what he beheld, and the partly unconscious desire to establish an identification for the reader as well, also contributed to the rhetorical structure. Agee's method then had to become complex.

Because his impressions and imaginative wanderings are central, the text must ultimately be approached as poetry. The most obvious instance of Agee's radically subjective language being simultaneously factual, lyrical, and rhetorical is found in his "Colon: Curtain Speech." This section is an extended meditation about how each tenant farmer's consciousness is formed from a complexity of sensations. Written like an interior monologue, the prose of the speech is tightly organized, and highly formal at times. The rhythms of the passage are those of a pulpit delivery, and what contributes to the pleasure of reading it is its predictability of sentence structure. Key words and phrases tie the passage together, and in addition there is a constantly recurring pitch and stress pattern. However, the basic device employed to convey the number of items impinging upon human consciousness is, as noted earlier, a poetic one, the extended use of metaphor. Five dominant images recur throughout this passage: crucifixion, flower, prison, water, and star. These different images are woven together in an evocation of Agee's feelings about these tenant farmers. Agee's experiments, which began with the reality, the desire to get at the facts, to be *un*imaginative, finally make it absolutely necessary that he also include the facts of his own imagination. That too is a reality, a fact.

Despite flaws, which are in most instances the extensions of merits, Agee's elaborate text, above all, manifests the dignity of particular tenant farmers, holy individuals, as beheld and imagined by the writer. What he experienced (even as he composed the text) Agee attempted to give back to his readers. With a combination of poetic imagination and a disciplined technique, he evokes the reality of what had been experienced, but in a much more complex way than others might have been willing to attempt.

A comment made by Agee several years after *Famous Men* had been published serves well as summary of what his intentions must have been as he wrote this text. Indeed, it could be used as a summary of his artistic philosophy: "I dislike allegory and symbolism which are imposed on and denature reality as much as I love both when they bloom forth and exalt reality."[14] *Famous Men* is a successful demonstration of the controlled use of many diverse approaches including near-verbal photography as well as the use of imagination to clarify and honor reality as experienced and remembered. Agee's decision to include his reactions and feelings within the text provides the necessary framework. That presence is what finally makes this image of tenant farming accurate, and of lasting value. It is a portrait of a time and the times of composition, and it is timeless.

Notes

[1] James Agee and Walker Evans, *Let Us Now Praise Famous Men* (Boston: Houghton Mifflin Company, 1941), p. xiv. Subsequent references to this edition will be made in the text.

[2] Autograph manuscript notebook, University of Texas Library, "Let Us Now Priase Famous Men," Notes, 40 1, n.d.*

[3] An undergraduate story published in the *Harvard Advocate*, "They That Sow in Sorrow Shall Reap," makes this clear. Note especially pp. 82-86, reprinted in *The Collected Short Prose of James Agee* (Boston: Houghton Mifflin Company, 1968).

[4] See J. Douglas Perry, Jr., "James Agee and the American Romantic Tradition" (Ph.D. dissertation, Temple University, 1968); Alfred Barson, "James Agee: A Study of Artistic Consciousness" (Ph.D. dissertation, University of Massachusetts, 1969); Peter H. Ohlin, *Agee* (New York: Ivan Obolensky, 1966).

[5] Kenneth Seib, *James Agee: Promise and Fulfillment* (Pittsburgh: University of Pittsburgh Press, 1968).

[6] William Stott, *Documentary Expression and Thirties America* (New York: Oxford University Press, 1973). See final chapters.

[7] A partial carbon-copy manuscript of *Famous Men*, now owned by the library of the University of Texas, reveals that "Part One" of an unused manuscript version of "Work," from which only "selections" were taken for the text, is an elaborate attempt to suggest the reiterative qualities of all physical labor. See also Alan Holder's comments in his "Encounter in Alabama: Agee and the Tenant Farmer," *Virginia Quarterly Review* (1966): 205-206.

[8] James Agee, *Letters of James Agee to Father Flye*, edited by James Harold Flye (New York: George Braziller, 1962), p. 104.

[9] Erik Wensberg, "Celebrating Adoration and Wonder," *Nation*, 26 November 1960, p. 418.

[10] Ralph W. Emerson, "The Poet," *The Selected Writings of R. W. Emerson* (New York: Modern Library, 1951), p. 326.

[11] Kenneth Burke, *Rhetoric of Motives* (New York: Prentice-Hall, 1950), p. 146; and Agee, *Letters*, pp. 114-115.

[12] Kenneth Burke, *Permanence and Change* (Los Altos, California: Hermes, 1954), p. 54.

[13] Marie Hochmuth Nichols, *Rhetoric and Criticism* (Baton Rouge: Louisiana State University Press, 1963), p. 85; and Burke, *Rhetoric of Motives*, p. 23.

[14] James Agee, *Agee on Film*, Volume 1 (Boston: Beacon Press, 1964), p. 288.

---

* Used with permission of the James Agee Trust.

III

Film and Society

Agee's Criticism as Insight Into Culture and the Problems of Making an Honest Film

The film criticism of Agee accomplishes two goals simultaneously. It provides a careful critique of films placed under his scrutiny, but incorporated with aesthetic and critical judgments are also found frequent indications of concern about the culture which generated the films. Throughout this criticism therefore one finds combined aesthetic and moral judgements, and if Agee is able to make a point clearer by reference to other aspects of culture, he does so. His concern as critic was never limited to a film's success or failure as a technical accomplishment. Agee was constantly aware of what a film revealed about its maker, its actors, and the culture which surrounded it.

Agee argued in much of his critical writing, and throughout *Let Us Now Praise Famous Men* that much could be, and indeed was, revealed through little. And when he came to write the commentary for *The Quiet One*, his initial filmwriting to be produced in 1948, he demonstrated that careful use of ordinary city streets and non-professional actors would evoke a mood impossible within a more contrived and artificial situation. Donald, the ten year old hero who is the focal point of that film, has no dialogue; but the film was made with such an awareness of how place causes loneliness that its very setting suggests the mood. This is caught through careful use of city scenes, and shots of Donald which reveal his state of mind. In *The Quiet One*, then, there is great respect for the actual.

Significantly, one of the fundamental issues which Agee discussed within his film criticism was a concern for the distortion which many films caused when attempting to represent actuality. Such misrepresentation perpetrated misbeliefs and caused many who watched films to make incorrect assumptions. And even more significantly, such films revealed many things about the culture which generated them. A related interest of Agee was his concern for the political

sphere and his consequent realization that art forms do have an
influence upon political belief and activity. This fact is evident throughout the film criticism, perhaps most obviously in Agee's elaborate
reviews for Chaplin's film *Verdoux*. While he approached *Verdoux*
from many different and often overlapping points of view his approach remained fundamentally political. He valued the fact that
Verdoux was oblique commentary upon our modern way of life.

Agee's criticism is clearly subjective, and at the base of his comments stand moral judgments. He insisted that he was an "amateur" in
the good sense of being an impartial observer, and maintained that
any film reveals its culture, but often the persons closest to it have
become unable to see. In his initial column he suggested that professional concern "with technique, with the box-office, with bad tradi-
tions, or simply with work, can blur, or alter the angle of ... judgment."
He announced that he would refuse to remove himself from his commentary, and thus he sought to avoid any simplistic view. The ending
of his opening (1941) column reveals this commitment and his awareness of the power of film to influence viewers. In a pattern which was
then to continue through all the criticism now gathered in *Agee on Film*
he wrote "I also urge that *Ravaged Earth*, which is made of Japanese
atrocities, be withdrawn until ... careful enough minds, ... shall have
determined whether or not there is any morally responsible means of
turning it loose on the public."[1] Whether such documentary footage
was technically good, or even accurate, remained secondary. Agee's
ethical judgment was the fundamental consideration. Similar judgments were incorporated through other columns in *The Nation* written
over a seven year period. His comments about Elizabeth Taylor (132)
or about hangovers (184) which some critics maintained got in the way
of his subject are essential. His reactions, as "amateur," are a combination of his sense of beauty and of the morally correct.

In his notes for an introduction to the photographer Helen
Levitt's *A Way of Seeing*, he once noted: "The mind and the spirit are
constantly formed by, and as constantly form, the senses, and misuse
or neglect the senses only at grave peril to every possibility of wisdom
and well-being."[2] Similarly a successful motion picture must honor
mind and senses; but a problem with so many films, as mass-produced
in the thirties and forties, was that their makers failed to combine an
awareness of how mind and spirit are affected.

Despite the limitations of their manufacture, Agee usually

perceived the good within the most ordinary of films. To be a film critic
forty years ago was a challenge, and Agee consistently found good
things to say about even mediocre films. The nineteen-forties was the
period before American audiences had ready access to European
films, and Hollywood functioned like a factory. Compounding the
problems of isolation and mass-production, the war apparently encouraged film makers to rely upon cliché. Thus, innumerable bad
films were produced. Yet Agee continually saw the possibilities of
film as a medium through which the modern artist could tap the
realistic, and make poetry. When Agee's movie criticism was collected
reviewers voiced a complaint that it lacked a consistent aesthetic. But
what unifies it is a veneration of reality and honor for the individual
present in all of Agee's most characteristic writing. His objections to
films produced during the forties in the factory-like conditions of Hollywood were objections to a form of entertainment (or art) which fell
far short of potentiality. Stereotypical ideas, predictable acting, cheap
sets, and ignorance of audience combined to dishonor the reality films
purported to present. Fundamental to this criticism, and recognized
so, is its "respect for human reality." Such respect "makes it the
function of art to picture as accurately and honestly as possible the
inherent beauty and immediacy of life."[3] Agee's comments about
Vittorio de Sica's *Shoeshine* reveal what he liked, but seldom found.
Shoeshine caught the "emotional directness" of the "story of two streets
boys who are caught almost by accident into the corrective machinery
of the state" (279). Its makers established a rapport with the audience,
and caught the spirit of a complexity. In working notes for this review
Agee noted how the makers of *Shoeshine*

> captured the dubious world of "social" art and turned it
> over to the humanistic tradition. The characterizations in
> *Shoeshine* are not deep or brilliant, yet you get more clearly
> than any movie I have seen, a realization of the complexity
> of interplay between the individual and the system, and his
> place in it. Both are accused, neither are accused; both are
> forgiven, nothing is forgiven.[4]

Within his criticism, and in the scripts he wrote as well, Agee
did not have the sense of freedom essential for the artist. He was either
dealing with "finished products" or materials adapted for the screen.
But his reviews articulate Agee's views, and what he admired in films

is related to his own writing which honors actuality. Above all Agee felt films should be made without a distorting artifice. He is disappointed with the machinery responsible for much of modern movies, machinery which made it almost impossible for ordinary common sense—closely related to artistic sense—to survive.

Much of what Agee felt wrong with movies is contrasted with what he was convinced was right with the best from the silent era when the visual image was predominant. His most sustained piece of criticism is an essay about silent comedies which, he argued, possessed an honesty which remained undistorted by any intermediary veneer. Silent comedies made audiences laugh, and this they did well. A mood of nostalgia is evoked as Agee reminisces about the silent era. Silent comedies were enjoyed because comedians knew how to suggest nuances without verbal assistance, but with the introduction of sound, good comedy deteriorated. "When a modern comedian gets hit on the head, for example, the most he is apt to do is look sleepy. When a silent comedian got hit on the head he seldom let it go so flatly.... It was his business to be as funny as possible physically, without the help or hindrance of words" (3). To communicate an appreciation of such accomplishments Agee relied upon a method of writing which suggested the silent images. He knew that his readers would be largely persons who had not seen silent films, or at least had not seen them recently. So in succinct fashion he provided phrases about actors such as Harold Lloyd who "smiled a great deal and looked like the sort of eager young man who might have quit divinity school to hustle brushes," or Buster Keaton who "carried a face as still and sad as a daguerreotype."

Agee's criteria for judging the success of silent comedy was laughter. The essay begins with definitions of the "titter, the yowl, the belly-laugh and the boffo." It was clear that modern comedy had come into an era of famine because most moviegoers only occasionally got beyond the yowl. Agee's essay suggests what thousands must have felt. He emphasizes that the best silent comedians were aware of what it means to be human but often that awareness was lost when more sophisticated techniques developed. Chaplin, Agee suggested, created a figure in the tramp who was: "as centrally representative of humanity, as many-sided and mysterious as Hamlet, and it seems unlikely that any dancer or actor can ever have excelled him in eloquence, variety or poignancy of motion" (9). Other comedians like

Harry Langdon could, perhaps in a more limited way than Chaplin, produce a laugh which also revealed "subtle emotional and mental processes." In one scene, Langdon, "watching a brazen showgirl change her clothes . . . sat motionless, back to camera, and registered the whole lexicon of lost innocence, shock, disapproval and disgust, with the back of his neck" (13). Such mastery of detail fascinated Agee. The silent films, he admits, were often shunned by "nice" people, "but millions of less pretentious people loved their sincerity and sweetness, their wild-animal innocence and glorious vitality." Agee states they "could not put these feelings into words, but they flocked to the silents" (6). In contrast, in many films of the forties both individual talent and a respect for the audience were lost. For such reasons, Agee's criticism was often heavily concerned with mistakes Hollywood incurred because it forgot that much could be revealed in little.

It appeared that the American film industry had the techniques for capturing all aspects of reality, but what was accomplished was barely lukewarm. In Agee's opinion many American films were "sick unto to death," because the possibilities for suggesting and recording reality were too frequently systematically ignored. To his mind, a blending of studio action, romantic characterizations, and documentary footage, as was the case with many "semi-documentaries" about the war, "chemically guaranteed the defeat of all possible reality" (67). He felt the big studios consistently underrated their audiences, and it disappointed him that spectators were treated as fools because he knew that they were more perceptive than assumed. Once he commented about a film which he theorized must have been designed with two endings: the ending of *The Curse of the Cat People* as produced, he theorized, must have slipped by the production office because it demanded more from its audience than oridnary box office fare. Agee had seen that film at a West Times Square theater, and the audience, one of the hardest imaginable to please, he noted, was satisfied. They did not feel they had been betrayed:

> Masquerading as a routine case of Grade B horrors—and it
> does very well at that job—the picture is in fact a brave,
> sensitive, and admirable little psychological melodrama
> about a lonely six year old girl . . . when the picture ended
> and it was clear beyond further suspense that anyone who
> had come to see a story about curses and werecats should-
> have stayed away, they clearly did not feel sold out; for an

> hour they had been captivated by the poetry and danger of
> childhood, and they showed it in their thorough applause.
> (85-86)

Usually Hollywood simply gave audiences what it assumed they
wanted. Thus, cliché and twistings of images resulted in films which
suggested nothing better than neurosis, a word Agee frequently employs. Such inappropriateness was unsatisfactory. More disturbing
was the fact that a bad film, like *Tender Comrade* "an infinitely degraded
and slickened *Little Women*" (90), was "likely to move, console, cor-
roborate, and give eloquence to" much of America. Such commerciali-
zation of bad taste exemplified the distorted emphasis and vulgarity
which made Agee feel especially ill at ease. For similar reasons he
laughed at the distortions within the Esther Williams' film *Bathing
Beauty* which unnaturally swarmed "with bathing suits and their
contents" (101). The inherent dishonesty of such productions insulted
audiences. Agee felt the same was true of Hollywood's insistence on
contriving inappropriate sets while the real world waited to be photographed. One clear example of his objections to bad sets and
improper locales is his reaction to *Dragon Seed*, an adaptation of a Pearl
S. Buck novel, and "an almost unimaginably bad movie." There, in an
attempt to suggest China, California hillsides were terraced and dyed
green for effect. And, as if that were not bad enough, Agee wrote, the
dialogue was atrocious: talk like "'the wind has brought the rain'
instead of 'it's raining,'" made the picture stilted. Characteristically,
Agee hastened to qualify that "finding a diction proper to so-called
simple folk is one of the most embarrassing . . . literary problems we
have set ourselves" (109).

Agee argued that film makers enjoyed no privilege to seek to
evoke a foreign culture when they were ignorant of it. The film, *The
North Star*, was an attempt to reflect the conduct of a small Russian
village on the border during the opening days of the war, but Agee felt
both audience and imagined village were mistreated: "every attempt
to use a reality brings the romantic juice and the annihilation of any
possible reality pouring from every gland" (57). To impose such false
interpretation made things worse: "The result is one long orgy of
meeching, sugaring, propitiation, which . . . enlists, develops, and
infallibly corrupts a good deal of intelligence, trust, courage, and
disinterestedness." Sometimes when realistic shots were incorpo-

rated in factory films they remained isolated, never to gather any "cinematic momentum" (84).

A concern with slickness, a finished product where all parts have a nice surface like "cosmetics on a cadaver" (92) often defeated any good qualities in a film. Agee insisted time after time, that ordinary beauty is lost when falsely made to look pretty; and for such reasons he often argued non-professional actors could do a better job of catching the immediacy of life than professionals; and therefore his objections to the use of professional actors, if non-professionals could more advantageously be employed, was an insight to which he kept returning. He was convinced that "art and actuality work on each other like live chemicals" (223), *if* a correct balance is maintained. But within the framework of many studio films, actors often could not pretend to be revealing real persons. (When Agee's criticism was collected, these ideas about amateur actors were often attacked. But, as he himself emphasized, his preference is for a language of images which reveals the real. If "acting" detracted from reality, then it should be sacrificed.) The chief interest of any good film maker should be to reveal reality, not to obscure it; and the Hollywood star-system obscured.

Given such objections, it is not surprising that Agee's preference was for a blending of realism and poetry. Reality was to be honored in a way that its individual parts manifested beauty. A successful film therefore was one which allowed the natural beauty to shine. Thus, Agee admired the combat film *Desert Victory* because it stood as "a clean, simple demonstration that creative imagination is the only possible substitute for the plainest sort of good sense—and is, after all, merely an intensification of good sense to the point of incandescence" (33). In this non-fiction film images had been respected for themselves, and the honesty of the film was its unifying factor. A few years later, writing about *San Pietro* directed by John Huston, Agee noted a similar success: "close to the essence of the power of moving pictures is the fact that they can give you things to look at, clear of urging or comment, and so ordered that they are radiant with illimitable suggestions of meaning and mystery." Huston's use of wordless children toward the end of that film was in Agee's opinion, a "great passage of war poetry" (164).

In Agee's view a successful film blended reality with imagination. He felt Andre Malraux's *Man's Hope* was such a success; but he also noted that while it was a commonplace "that movie and musical form are closely related," few films demonstrated awareness of such a relationship. In *Man's Hope* all the parts bl_nded together—even the shots which suggested an "excess of energy," "letting things and movements into [the] frame which have nothing to do with the central action . . . little things which brilliantly lock men and their efforts and feelings into the exact real place and time of day" (240). It is not surprising that Agee most admired films which suggested the complexity of life itself. His admiration for a blending of different images, combining the expected and unexpected, is basic to his admiration for Vigo's *Zero de Conduite*. There the subjective and the objective, the fantastic reality of the subconscious along with the conscious, blended. Agee felt it was perfectly approprite for a film maker to incorporate several different methods as long as all of the methods were attempts to get at the truth. Agee's defense of still another film makes clear his approval of Vigo's film. He had noted a shiftiness of style; but he insisted "if you accept that principle in Joyce or in Picasso, you will examine with interest how brilliantly it can be applied in moving pictures and how equally promising" (75). His fundamental criterion for an honest film was its freshness and vitality, a spirit close to actual experience. He felt this was accomplished in Rossellini's *Open City* where the performance of Anna Magnani was near "the poetic-realistic root of attitude from which the grand trunk of movies at their best would have to grow" (195). It is clear why he disliked films which seemed to be only imitations of imitations.

His technical observations are always closely related to the aesthetic he outlined in his call for poetic realism. A good director should honor his audience by making his film more than just a passive instrument. Agee knew that the effective use of a single shot, the judicious use of cutting, stop-shots, slow motion, repetition, etc., all contributed to the total effect. Properly used such procedures help a director to mirror reality. Similarly, the use of actual localities rather than contrived sets, proper use of background music, and color to support mood could contribute to the rhythm of a work.

One film which illustrated the successful uses of technique blended with a respect for reality was *Farrebique* which chronicled the lives of ordinary French farmers. Its director, George Rouquier realized "that, scrupulously handled, the camera can do what nothing else in the world can do; . . . record unaltered reality." Agee's admiration of *Farrebique* is a clear indication of his guiding aesthetic. The honesty of that documentary resulted in more than documentation:

> One could watch the people alone, indefinitely long, for the inference of his handling of them, to realize that moral clearness and probity are indispensable to the work of this kind, and to realize with fuller contempt than ever before how consistently in our time so-called simple people, fictional and non-fictional are betrayed by artists and by audiences. . . . (297)

Other critics charged that *Farrebique* was repetitious. Agee agreed that indeed this was so, in exactly the same way as "the imitation and counterpoint and recurrence in a Mozart symphony are repetitious, and somewhat near as satisfying" (298).

Implied, and sometimes categorically spelled out was Agee's moral stance which supports this criticism. He repeatedly insisted that motion pictures possessed enormous power to reveal the depths of the human condition and he became angry when such possibilities were ignored. Huston's *San Pietro* was a success because of its honesty. Its footage was shot during combat; veteran soldiers were participants. The film was shot; then developed in Washington, and only on return to the States had Huston edited it. At the heart of what Huston accomplished was attention to the complexity and interaction of battle, its participants, the villages, and nature itself. Agee felt the film possessed clarity and moral integrity because it grew out of something Huston and his crew clearly respected.

Agee maintained that no one had a right to make a film about something he did not understand. Yet misunderstanding and its attendant errors were fascinating to him. Often he criticized the cinema as a revelation of our culture; and occasionally he even referred to films as collective dreams.[5] Even a not particularly good-picture revealed facts of the culture which generated it. Writing about *The Blue Dahlia*, he said it is "neatly stylized and synchronized, and as uninterested in moral excitement, as a good ballet; it knows its own weight and size perfectly and carries them gracefully and without self-importance." In its uninsistent way "it does carry a certain amount of social criticism," for it "crawls with American types; and their mannerisms and affectations, and their chief preoccupations . . . " (203). Agee wanted film audiences to develop their abilities to see such things.

human potentialities

The problem of course, was that most had little capability to discriminate.

Good films, made and viewed in the proper spirit could suggest potentialities lost and the possibilities man has for gain. Such insights remain at the heart of Agee's desideratum. He once wrote "The films I most eagerly look forward to will not be documentaries but works of pure fiction, played against and into, and in collaboration with unrehearsed and uninvented reality" (237). Such expectations account for Agee's admiration of Chaplin's *Monsieur Verdoux,* a film he regarded as a statement about man's loss of individualism. In order to preserve his family the character Verdoux was driven to extreme measures. To keep his family enshrined in isolation, Verdoux became a professional murderer, marrying, then killing women of means for their money. Such actions were necessary to survive at all in modern society. *Verdoux,* Agee suggested, was "a metaphor for the modern personality." Interestingly this film could not even be seen in the United States until a few years ago.

Agee felt that *Verdoux* was successful because, as in all of Chaplin's work, the best elements of primitive and civilized art blended in a way that never weakened each other. *Verdoux* contained scenes of hilarious humor, but always enforced by seriousness. Chaplin's film indicted modern civilization, but it did so by demonstrating how inextricably bound good and evil remain. It was a success because it was carefully made, but it also made a clear moral statement.

Agee's criticism prepared him to write screenplays, and it is not surprising that his first full-length efforts in the late-forties included a projected film for Chaplin. Never finished, that utopian film was imagined to take place after the "ultimate bomb" had reduced modern civilization to ashes. Approximately ten years earlier Agee had completed a screenplay called "The House" wherein he combined many techniques, from stop-shots to surrealism, to provide an indictment of contemporary society. While neither of these films were produced they remain an important source of ideas, and make one basic thing about Agee's theories clear: language is minimized in his plans for films. Whole sequences are planned which rely only upon the visual. What Agee seems to have realized, thirty or forty years in advance of many film makers, is that language can be a barrier instead of a help in communication.

Ironically, however, when Agee wrote a screenplay he used a great deal of explicit language. His own screenplays might be described as the product of a frustrated director because he used so much language to suggest what he knew might be done with film. *The Night of the Hunter* and *The African Queen* are two of his better-known adaptations, both successful because he was able to create a mood with the scenario. Those moods are built up by means of focus on the immediate. Thus in *The African Queen* the opening sequence, considerably more detailed than in C. S. Forester's novel, is planned with the precision of a good documentary, rather than with the approach of a melodrama. The same must be said of Agee's use of short stories by Stephen Crane as basis for movies.

What Agee sought through all his criticism, and in his writing of screenplays, was successful combination of poetry and reality which would honor the real world, not distort it. His detailed comments of admiration, as well as his successful screenplays, still stand today as a record of how others could perfect methods.

Notes

[1] *Agee on Film*, Volume 1 (New York: McDowell, Obolensky, 1958), pp. 23-24. All subsequent references are noted parenthetically.

[2] The notes for *A Way of Seeing* are catalogued as: "Unidentified manuscript, working draft," n.d., University of Texas Library. This material is gratefully used with the permission of the James Agee Trust.

[3] *Agee* (New York: Obelensky, 1966), p. 125.

[4] Autograph working draft with autograph emendations (25 pp.) (1947 October) University of Texas Library.

[5] See Agee's discussion of *Mission to Moscow; Since You Went Away; Hail the Conquering Hero;* and *The Birth of a Nation* (pp. 37, 107, 117, and 313) in *Agee on Film*, Volume 1.

Chaplin's Screenplay as Statement About Society

I

James Agee was convinced that Chaplin was a consummate artist. He could, and did, compare him with Shakespeare and Beethoven. Thus, it is not surprising that he wanted to write a screenplay for him. Robert Fitzgerald, in his "Memoir" about Agee, writes, "he had wanted for years to do a scenario for Chaplin; whether he ever did more than imagine it, I have been unable to find out."[1] Agee not only imagined it. He wrote a good portion, and while the fragments are perhaps not especially important as scenario, they do provide valuable insight into both Agee's admiration for Chaplin, and his concept of the individual in a society locked into the irrationality of herd instincts, combined with an awe of modern science. At what time Agee sketched his ideas for a projected scenario for Chaplin is unknown. It probably was before he met Chaplin in 1951, a year when they spent some "30 or 50 evenings" in conversation.[2]

There is no detailed record of their conversations. But in a letter to Father Flye, Agee mentions his enjoyment in "seeing a great deal of Chaplin and his wife."[3] Some months later he explained that he had spent many "evenings talking alone most of the night with Chaplin," and regretted that he had recorded only a little of those evenings "in a couple or three letters to Mia. . . ," his wife.[4] Without a doubt Agee and Chaplin must have talked about the famous *Monsieur Verdoux* (1947). That film was a crucial part of Chaplin's career, and it had been recognized by Agee as a work of fundamental importance. *Verdoux* had provoked a three-part extended review, Agee's longest film commentary, in *The Nation*.[5] Many years later Dwight Macdonald sought to provide some explanation of why Agee had been so taken with *Verdoux*. He suggested finally that "the appeal of Verdoux may be political rather than cinematic."[6] The fact that the film must have seemed valuable as political commentary may have caused Agee to think about other such possibilities for Chaplin.

Agee saw *Verdoux* as a statement about man's loss of individualism. To achieve a semblance of dignity modern man has been driven to take extreme, perhaps insane, measures. To preserve his family it becomes necessary for the film character Verdoux to be at continual war with society. He is driven to becoming a professional murderer, killing women of means for their money, "in order to preserve intact ... those aspects of the personality which are best and dearest."[7] In the film Verdoux enshrines his family in isolation from his crimes; but he does so to provide them with security. Agee wrote in his working notes for the review that:

> if the film is regarded as a metaphor for the personality, and through that ... as a metaphor for the personality as the family as business as war as civilization as murder, then this is certain: if the man and his wife had honored their marriage with more than their child, the murders would never have been committed, the paralysis would never have imposed itself ... all three would have lived as one in the poverty for which the wife was forlorn: in the intactness of soul and the irresponsibility of that anarchic and immortal lily of the field, the tramp, the most humane and most nearly complete among religious figures our time has evolved; whom for once in his life Chaplin set aside to give his century its truest portrait of the upright citizen.

The theme of Chaplin's *Verdoux* was recognized by Agee as "the greatest and most appropriate to its time" because it took up "the bare problem of surviving at all in such a world as this." Therefore Agee, who calls for a recognition of the individual throughout all of his writings, recognized *Verdoux* as a basic statement about man's loss of dignity. He felt the film was a superb metaphor for man in modern society.

Other critics objected to Chaplin's change of roles in this controversial film, but Agee argued that the film was a continuation of Chaplin's earlier work, and that Verdoux as a metaphor for modern society was but the evolution of the figure of the tramp. He suggested that "very young children fiercely object to even minor changes in a retold story. Older boys and girls are not, as a rule, respected for such extreme conservatism."

As Agee began to write scenarios, his view of contemporary society, his abhorrence of the atomic bomb, his life-long admiration of Chaplin, and (perhaps) his fascination with *Verdoux* seem to have converged to suggest the tramp as an appropriate vehicle for a vision of a new society where the individual might again play a significant role. The projected screenplay "Scientists and Tramps" was sketched as a suggestion of what could happen should man trigger the "ultimate Bomb." If our civilization, apparently on the brink of blowing itself up, did so, then the individualism embodied in Chaplin's tramp could serve as the symbol of a revitalizing force. Agee's notes for "Scientists and Tramps" indicate his fears about the society following World War II. The horror of man's first use of atomic energy was an important aspect of his consciousness, a horror projected most forcefully in his satire "Dediction Day," a report of the commemoration ceremony for the monument erected in honor of the first historic use of atomic energy. There the humor is macabre. The victims of the holocaust are imagined as those given the "privilege" of tending an eternal flame which commemorates the occasion of man's first use of atomic power.[8] In the projected screenplay Agee imagines society reconstructing itself after the "ultimate bomb" had been dropped; but the mood of the projected film was to be without the bitterness of "Dedication Day." It is an attempt to suggest what might be possible for man if he could, again, act as an individual. The problem of individualism is at the core of Agee' concern in this scenario. Implied is a question, is it possible for an individual to retain dignity in a society where faith had been placed in science to the degree that men no longer were willing to assume the burden of thinking for themselves?

II

If an atomic bomb leveled the United States and a new civilization emerged from its ruins, Agee saw the individualism which Chaplin's tramp represented as an important symbol for hope. A film about the possibilities of reconstruction could be both a comedy which relied upon all of the skill Agee admired in Chaplin's work, and a commentary about contemporary America.

The film was to take place following the nuclear destruction of much of the world. Parts of it were to be made in Manhattan, and near there the "Tramp's Community" was to be imaginatively established. The scientist's camp was to be not so far away, at Philadelphia. The story line began in the following manner: After "no more than five minutes" of "comic political-scientific prologue" the "ultimate Bomb" is dropped. Opening scenes were to be incorporated depicting the world-wide devastation. Then Chaplin does the first sequence as a "tremendous solo . . . wandering in a dead metropolis."[9] On the second day the tramp is piecing together "a way of living" when he discovers a baby, all but new born. On the following day he encounters still another survivor, a young woman, and the opening three-day sequence ends at nightfall "before they . . . realize their fortune, the wonder of being alive and of being a family."

Then glimpses were to be provided of other types who have also survived. "Diplomats, who were spotted in the prologue . . . , keep right on trying to be diplomats. Still more important, scientists keep right on trying to be scientists." The scientists would also, almost immediately, begin piecing together a new civilization. The re-emergence of the two divergent ways of life would provide the basic development for the rest of the film.

The opening scenes would have been a combination of the best aspects of Chaplin's humanism combined with an implied criticism of the technocracy which produced the Bomb. It does not seem accidental that a policeman was chosen as the "first victim of the bomb." The tramp stumbles upon the blasted figure:

> He is a very irate and brutal cop, running right foot and
> night stick raised, on his face a glowing ferocity. The force,
> light and heat of the bomb have reduced and flattened him
> to a slightly distorted photograph against the stone wall of
> the building.

Agee saw that when such a bomb was dropped the "authorities" would have met their match. But he realized that they, and all the powers of science and government, would have been obliterated only for a little while. And the conclusion of the projected film certainly makes this clear. It ends with the scientists again very much in control.

Agee's sketch, in addition to the prologue and the opening scenes with the tramp and scientists, suggests how an alternation between the two camps would follow. The gradual ascension of the scientists once again to power would be a basic part of the film. The plans were for the film to alternate from the "Chaplinesque" to the scientific. Thus, there would have been shifts between "The Forces of Good ('maturity,' 'responsibility,' 'social-mindedness,' all the beliefs that have made civilization what it is), as contrasted with simple child-like survival." Agee suggested the scientists would be "far gone" in abstraction. And this helps them to keep on "improving on the science of destruction" and to reestablish contact "with their kind all over the world." Finally:

> It is they who gather in the stragglers and the eccentrics, including the whole of Chaplin's little civilization; and it is they who end the picture in triumph, with an even more terrible bomb up their sleeves and even more terrible destruction just around the corner from the last shots in the picture.

Other scene outlines indicate how the scientists would be portrayed during those hours after the detonation of the bomb when they were still unsure of its total effect. These men, with their immense scientific capabilities, are able to recover much of their original powers within a short span of time. Yet at the same time they remain unsure whether it would be prudential to touch their women. Always contrasted with such scenes is the fact that the Tramp is very calmly going about the business of reestablishing a community.

Some of the additional sketched scenes include moments when the scientists reveal their ineptitude, or selfishness, as contrasted with scenes about the other emergent group which reveal forgotten skills rediscovered because of love and care for other persons. The Tramps' community is altogether different from anything the modern world is used to: "The one concern is, does my own enjoyment deprive or hurt another; and that is also one of the few laws." Agee suggested that in this imaginary community

> it is found that nearly everybody prefers to work. . . . The wages are barter or work in exchange. . . . [And] it is explained that there is nothing intrinsically evil about machinery, synthetic substances, labor saving etc., but that once they are admitted, chain reactions seem inevitably to set in which get far beyond human control. Plenty of

> people remember, wistfully, the pleasures of auto-driving,
> for instance. But the making of even one auto, and the use
> of power, involves too many people to be good in the long
> run ... though machines are neither good nor evil, much is
> lost when personal skill and strength are lost.

How to dramatize all of this, and how to suggest that in a "Utopian" community all of the problems were not solved, was finally something Agee knew would be extremely difficult. The film was to be a satire and thus parts of it would be extremely funny. But at the same time he knew that "an all-important aspect of the picture [was] that utopias are not never-never-lands; that many of the sorrows and needs of individuals are never to be salved. . . ."

In view of what Agee felt about the projected film as a whole, the final sequence of the picture is not really surprising. The care with which he sketched out its inevitability is an accomplishment. Here he combined the tragedy of a fate which must befall the individualism of the Tramp with irony which creates satire—amusing, and frightening at the same time. For there was no way for an individual such as a Tramp to be tolerated in a society like the one being rebuilt. It was only a matter of time before he had to be eliminated. The final sequence was to include a confrontation between the two camps, described in general terms, in the following way:

> One by one they all move over to the scientists' camp. Some
> of the last few speak to him, take his hand. The burden of
> their explanation is that they are heartsick to say so (and
> they really are), but it is hopelessly impractical. If only all
> people felt as he did, of course.—But they *do*, the tramp
> insists, in their heart they do! If only they had the courage,
> the trust, ... [Finally the tramp] stands alone now. He
> bows silent to the Scientists, tips his hat to some woman
> and starts away. Two of the scientists . . . whispering
> (general idea: that man *could* be dangerous; radio the word
> along to pick him up when it won't be noticed).
>
> Old Glory climbs the remains of the Empire State, band
> plays the Star Spangled Banner, while all stand in solemn
> joy; we last see the Tramp walking west on the G. W.
> bridge. The anthem comes thinly through somebody's
> portable radio. He is alone, walking west into Sunset.
> Walking east, escorted by arm-banded Scientific police-
> men, is an extremely variegated representation of the

whole human race, combed from the ruins, converging,
hopefully upon the birth of the new world. The tramp
smiles at them sportingly, they give him a black stare. By
degrees these stares become hostile, and his whole de-
meanor becomes older and lovelier. At the same time,
more and more like the old tramp—so that he picks up
great gayety of life of his own as he moves out. As he
changes, everyone sees him more and more as a rank and
possibly dangerous outsider. One of the policemen picks
up the scientist's message on his little radio. He gives the
tramp the eye and speaks to another cop. The tramp eyes
them back. They start after him, walking. He walks faster.
They walk faster. He trots. They trot. He breaks into a
headlong sprint and disappears, off the end of the bridge
with law and order in hot pursuit.

The only part of "Scientists and Tramps" which appears to be
near complete is the introductory speech to be delivered by the "Grand
Old Man" of democracy, but it sets the tone for everything which was
to follow. This speech, which Agee wrote to be delivered against a
buildup of film clips from newsreels is a parody of American politics,
and an indictment of the guillible American public. The speech runs
to ten manuscript pages and in it the speaker insists that he respects
the individualism that makes democracy great "in its place." The
speech builds to a crescendo which makes it clear that no deviation
from established patterns is to be tolerated at all. Respect for the
individual hardly exists, and it becomes clear that much of what
passes for democratic action is in reality the result of a fear that
individual thinking may result in trouble for the masses. As parody
this speech ranks with the best humor Agee wrote. The alternating
voices of "Time" and "Individualism" prepare the way for the "Grand
Old Man":

Voice of Time
... for better or for worse, civilization is knitted together by
the cooperation of individuals in groups, of men and
women who forget their little differences for the sake of the
many. That is the meaning of democracy.

Voice of Individualism
The death knell of democracy, you mean!

As Agee conceived it, then, the beginning of the film would have been

political satire which would have used as sound track a speech, a
harangue, delivered by the voice of a caricatured politician. The words
would have spun out in a verbal explosion at the beginning and
combined with an explosion of still shots, newsreel clips, and acted
scenes which would have established the mood of the world as it
approached nuclear catastrophe. The lengthy speech, apparently
complete, is a successful parody of a politician's way of speaking. But
it is also an indictment of the many things which Americans are
willing to accept without really thinking. It is, of course, that kind of
non-thinking which places man on the brink of blowing himself off
the earth.

"Scientists and Tramps," as projected, might well have been
impossible to execute in a single film. This ambitious project would
have combined an appreciation of the virtues of individualism with a
celebration of the human soul, along with satire about the political
foibles of twentieth-century America. Agee was convinced that modern
man, so reliant upon science, had forgotten how to act as a separate
person. In the exchange planned for the beginning of this film the
"Voice of Individualism" laments: "We have forgotten how to think as
single individuals, and how to feel moral responsibility as single
individuals. We think and pass moral judgment in groups." However,
Agee is fully aware of the immense difficulties he confronted in
finding a way of

> *dramatizing fully enough,* how [the tramp] has his strong
> influence on people. I am sure of it, that people coming
> slowly together out of the shock and horror and finding
> this childlike man, surviving bravely and well, could
> rediscover the childlikeness in themselves and live accord-
> ingly. . . .

Perhaps Agee's hopes for the film are best compared to those of
utopian fiction. In times of cultural crises men tend to seek refuge in
the past, in the future, or in various kinds of psychic withdrawal. This
projected film could be interpreted as a retreat from the horrors of the
contemporary world. A similar pattern was followed by Agee in the
conception and execution of his autobiographical novel, *A Death in the
Family.* In fact, in all of his writing he celebrates moments of innocence
as they are overshadowed by the complexities of living. Such is his accomplishment in *Let Us Now Praise Famous Men* where he chronicles

the lives of tramp-like common tenant farmers. The sketch for "Scientists and Tramps" is only a beginning; yet its insight into the difficulty of maintaining one's integrity in a society such as ours remains important. Written over forty years ago, it is prophetic.

Notes

[1] *The Collected Short Prose of James Agee* (Boston: Houghton Mifflin Company, 1968), p. 50.

[2] *Letters of James Agee to Father Flye* (New York: George Braziller, 1962), p. 191.

[3] *Letters*, p. 185.

[4] *Letters*, p. 192.

[5] *Agee on Film*. Volume 1 (New York: Grosset and Dunlap, 1967), pp. 252-262.

[6] Dwight Macdonald, "Chaplin, Verdoux, and Agee." *Esquire*, LXIII (April 1965), p. 33.

[7] *Monsieur Verdoux*, autograph manuscript working draft with autograph revisions (1947 May-June) now in the possession of The University of Texas Library. This and other unpublished material is gratefully used with the permission of the James Agee Trust.

[8] "Dedication Day, rough sketch for a moving picture." *New Directions*, No. 10, edited by James Laughlin (New York: New Directions, 1948), pp. 252-263.

[9] This manuscript is in the possession of The University of Texas Library and is catalogued as "Unidentified television or screenplay," autograph manuscript working draft with autograph revisions (c. 1948), 64 pp.

IV

Honoring Memories from Life

Regional Focus in the Fiction

As early as his student days of Phillips Exeter academy in the 1920's James Agee relied upon experience of Tennessee to provide background for poetry and fiction. Some of that apprentice fiction and drama possesses a mountain setting; and the employment of biography, for him a combination of urban and rural, was to remain of significance in later writing. For instance, in the spring of 1936, the first extended free time which he experienced after college, some of the best writing he produced was dependent onTennessee backgrounds. He was on leave from *Fortune* magazine, and one of his projects was the sketch "Knoxville: Summer of 1915" (later used by editors as a prelude for *A Death in the Family*). In that sketch Agee recreated moments when he and family relaxed in the evening as they reclined on quilts behind their house. These were moments when the peacefulness of nature blended with the quiet of the city. Each family member was recalled, and emphasis was placed upon the memory of the father, someone who had come to the city from the mountains. A similar pattern emerges in the novel *A Death in the Family*, planned largely as a memorial to Agee's father, but written toward the end of his life. The autobiographical "1928 Story," written at about the same time as *A Death* and *The Morning Watch*, are also demonstrations that as Agee grew older it became increasingly satisfying for him to fictionalize autobiographical remembrance.

But much of his earlier writing had incorporated a strong element of autobiography. His now classic account of tenant farming, *Let Us Now Praise Famous Men* (1941), is as much about Agee the reporter as it is about the farmers with whom he lived. He reports events as witnessed, but with the fact in mind that he felt a kinship with the people about whom he wrote. He was able to associate much of his background with the atmosphere of the Alabama he reported. He makes the point that given a different conjunction of circumstances he might have been born into a similar way of life. A positive value of *Let Us Now Praise Famous Men* is this autobiographical aspect.

Perhaps the clearest indication of the relationship between past and present, biography and immediacy, in *Famous Men* is a section where Agee allows his memory to reconstruct earlier times recalled about a dull Sunday afternoon when he drove from a small town toward a particular farm, and in the process remembered having spent similar afternoons at both of his grandparents' houses. The contrast is striking. The memory of the city house is that of an eleven-year-old who lay on the porch floor wondering about his intense loneliness. The contrasting memory is of a country farm, up in the mountains; the remembrance of torment is balanced with a more peaceful remembrance. Agee recalled being in the spring house. There he played, enjoying its coolness. He experienced:

> the odor of shut darkness, cold, wet wood, the delighting smell of butter; and standing in this spring, the crocks, brimmed with unsalted butter and with cream and milk; [a] place... shut behind me, but slit through with daylight, but the lighting comes as from a submerged lamp, that is, from the floor of the spring of which half is beyond shelter of the house.[1]

These memories are presented within the context of Agee's report of a listless Sunday afternoon when he had driven from small town to small town seeking diversion, only to be frustrated. He then drove out on a country road to look for the farm families about whom he was later to write—and suddenly, in their presence, he felt refreshed. His frustration was gone and it "was as if, to this thirsting man ... the sky became somber and opened its heart." Seeking a metaphor to suggest his feelings, he described drinking from a stream deep in the woods, and this metaphor reminded him of the satisfaction he had earlier derived from being in the mountain spring house as a child.

It has often been assumed that Agee spent five years at St. Andrew's Boarding School, from 1919 to 1924, and immediately continued schooling at Phillips Exeter Academy and Harvard. But summers were spent in Knoxville, and some visiting with rural relatives probably took place. Also an additional year was spent living in Knoxville in 1924-1925 as a high school student. These periods allowed the young writer to familiarize himself with the surrounding countryside. Interviews with persons who knew the Agee family indicate that they enjoyed going for rides in the country.[2] Also notes for *A Death in the Family* indicate Agee contemplated possibly writing additional fictional episodes which would have been about other country outings similar to his completed account of the visit to the great-grandmother.[3]

Agee knew that his personality was a composite of his father's mountain heritage and the somewhat more sophisticated urban family background from which his mother came. To do honor to the memory of the father's mountain heritage necessitated reconstruction, at least by implication, of how the father's biography had contributed to a way of life which the young Rufus experienced. Agee therefore inferred what his father might have felt as he lived in Knoxville, removed from the rural surroundings which he had known earlier.

The poem "In Memory Of My Father," first published in 1937, also draws on this "memory." The mood of the poem evokes the quiet of night in the country as it settles over a mountain. Such peacefulness and darkness cannot be found in a city. A city is disturbed by noises and by artificially created lights. Way back in the mountains when night comes the family is all alone; but that solitude is natural:

> Mile on mile in mountain folded valley
> fallen   valley lies
> Eyes fixed on silence small owls preach
> forlorn   forlorn:

This quiet is full of the sounds of nature.

> The metal thrill of frog and cricket
> thousands in the weltered grass.[4]

In "In Memory Of My Father" Agee imaginatively returns to the mountain background he closely associated with his father's origins. As an evocation of an evening's quiet, the poem suggests how this was a natural occurrence which reminded man of his harmony with the earth. At night everything becomes quieter, the countryside peaceful. Children lie quietly in their beds. The field, actively worked by day, is undisturbed:

sweet tended field, now mediate your
children, child, in your smokesweet
        quilt, joy in your dreams,
and father, mother: whose rude hands
        rest you mutual of the
flesh: rest in your kind flesh well:
And thou most tender earth:
Lift through this love thy creatures
        on the light.

This poem foreshadows the contemplative methods of *Let us Now Priase Famous Men*; and the imagined child, happy in its bed, is much like the young Rufus of *A Death in the Family* who is comforted by his father as he drifts off to sleep. In both this early poem and in the novel, Agee constantly reminds his reader that men are children of nature. As man has become more sophisticated culturally, it becomes easier to forget this fact. Urban man has become more dependent on machines and institutions, and has developed more faith in progress, rather than a trust in nature. Agee felt that his father had been a victim of such progress, and his novel demonstrates how many of the father's characteristics were admirable because they had a rural origin; and he was not at home in an urban setting.

As Agee matured he became increasingly aware that he had become what he was because of his mother's influence and because of the absence of a father associated with a rural, less sophisticated, background. In *A Death in the Family* the religion (and religiosity) of the fictional mother is a basic ingredient in her reaction to the death of the husband, Jay. The fictional father is appealing precisely because he seems to be more independently strong. The inference is that Rufus, the son, will become reliant upon formal religion after his father's death. The naturalness and openness, fundmentally rural qualities of the father, will then be missed.

Agee wanted to write of his earliest relationship with his father. By reconstructing the years of childhood he showed how the father's presence promised to be a positive influence for Rufus's formation. A basic theme of *A Death in the Family* is the difficulty of feeling at home. This is fundamental in the opening chapter as Jay and Rufus walk home together from the movies. The same motif appears in the "darkness" chapter when Jay sings to his son; a manuscript version of that chapter is longer because Jay remembers his own childhood, and muses about man's inability to return to an earlier situation. This motif is connected with both Jay's ironic journey to his father's bedside which leads to his own accidental death, and with the family's Sunday outing to La Follette. It is also reiterated at the closing of the novel when Rufus walks with his Uncle Andrew. In each of these instances Agee emphasizes the difficulty of maintaining continuity in a rapidly changing context.

One of the basic ideas throughout the book is clearly developed in the opening chapter when Rufus and his father feel close to each other. Agee suggests that one cannot easily feel at ease with the responsibilities of living, but at the same time, it is necessary to accept frustration. It is clear from the opening sequence that Jay cannot feel completely comfortable as a family man who lives in the city—with all the attendant responsibilities. But he accepts this difficulty. Of course, Agee makes no overt statement to this effect. But after enjoying Charlie Chaplin and William S. Hart, Rufus and Jay begin their walk home and stop, as they often did, at a saloon for a quick drink. They are barely through the door before Jay is looking up and down at faces to see if anyone is present from his home area, the Powell River Valley. He seeks companionship and some continuity with his past. That evening he finds none; and during the rest of the walk home words are not necessary for Rufus to sense that the father is not at ease. At such times father and son often sat for a few moments on a limestone outcropping to enjoy their solitude. This was a quiet which allowed them to feel close to nature and to each other; however, even then the peacefulness was periodically interrupted by the noises of the city. The implication is that a man like Jay can never be completely happy in the city.

In the second chapter of the novel when a telephone call comes in the middle of the night, and Jay decides he must go to his father's bedside, Agee suggests that there was a distinct pleasure in his anticipation of the drive up into mountain country. Mary, his wife, senses this too; (perhaps subconsciously) she insists that he eat a good breakfast before he leaves. She cooked eggs with more pepper than usual and he complimented her.

> She was pleased. Not more than half consciously, she had done this because within a few hours he would doubtless eat again, at home [his parents']. For the same reason she had made the coffee unusually strong. And for the same reason she felt pleasure in standing at the stove while he

ate, as mountain women did.[5]

As Jay drives out into the countryside he feels relieved to be rid of the city, exhilarated; and when the ferryman takes the Model T over the river, the scene suggests that Jay is being delivered from an alien urban existence.

It is not accidental that Agee planned this episode to include a description of mountaineers on the other side of the river. They were waiting to go into town to market. The faces of both man and woman were "the sad, deeply lined faces of the profound country which seemed ancient even in early maturity."[6] They had called for the ferryman, but he had not heard them. Jay realizes that they would be late for the market. "They had probably waited for the ferry as much as a couple of hours. They would be hopelessly late." Jay extends his sympathy to the wagoner and his wife because he knows that in a sense these mountaineers were drawn into the city just as he himself had been, and its promise will not bring fulfillment. No wonder that once Jay is "across the river . . . the cabins looked difficult to him, a little older and poorer and simpler, a little more homelike . . . the air smelled different." This was his country and he enjoyed returning.

Jay is what he is largely because of a rural background, and his son, Rufus, could have been influenced. The picture of Rufus's parents combines the best qualities of both, apparent when Jay and Mary, separately, sing to Rufus. The father loved to sing the old country songs. But Rufus also remembered how his parents sang together, and how beautifully his mother's clear voice combined with Jay's. He also noticed when she tried to sound like a country singer she could not. Rufus "liked both ways very much and best of all when they sang together and he was there with them. . . ." But the father's influence is lost.[7]

One of the chapters focuses on an evening when Jay went to Rufus's room because he was afraid of the dark. Jay comforted Rufus and then sang. The singing put the father into a meditative mood, and then he remembered his own childhood and the fact that his mother must have comforted him in a similar way.

This was a section of the book which must have interested Agee because he wrote pages of detailed variant manuscript. Agee's editors excluded this variant from the composite novel. The more detailed variant paragraphs provide a glimpse of how important the mountain background seemed for Agee's fictional Jay. The thoughts reflected are similar to those of three short paragaphs printed in the novel, but in the detailed manuscript Agee places more emphasis on Jay's thoughts about childhood on a farm in the mountains:

> *If he was right there he couldn't have seen it any clearer. The big old shaggy cedar was blowing in the sunshine and it looked like it was full of sparks. He could see just how the limestone jutted out of the clay. He could even smell wood-smoke. He could see how the square logs of the wall lay on top of each other side by side, ever so sleepy-looking and stout and still in the shakey light of the fire and the dark-brown light of the turned-down lamp. And there was his mother's face. It was young and round and it leaned over close above him.*
>
> *He could feel her ridgy hand on his forehead, pushing back the hair and just stroking his forehead, easy, and she was talking real low,* don't you fret Jim, now don't you fret. *She was saying* get on to sleep now. There ain't nothing to be afeared about. *She was saying* Maw's right here son. Paw's right here. Now get on back to sleep now. Don't you fret. *And she was smiling.*
>
> *She had a quilt pinned around her shoulders, and it smelled of smoke, hickory, and oak, and pine.*
>
> *Any house that didn't have that smoky smell, it just didn't smell like home.*
>
> *He could see the chimney up against the end of the place and the fireplace inside, both at the same time. Some of the chimney was stone and the rest was made of* [illegible word] *saplings and clay.*
>
> *Her face was real young but it was already full of lines and gouges. Her hand was the prettiest there was but it felt soapy.*
>
> *He could see the fire lazing in the stove fireplace and kind of cussing to itself under its breath, the way green wood does, and the sparks crawling along the soot of the back like a starry night. Just sixteen when I was born.*
>
> *He could see the humps of bread under the hot ashes. That's how bread tastes the best. Just blow the ashes off of it and eat it so hot it burns you.*
>
> *He could see strings of peppers hanging from a rafter, and strings of corn. He could see the marks of the axe in the oak logs of the wall and a place where the clay chinking had worked out and a tow sack had been prodded in. Just a girl. Don't you fret. Wasn't hardly no time since she was just a baby. Lord God and before his time, before he was ever dreamt of*

in this world, she must have laid like that under her own mother's hand or her daddy's, gentling her forehead Don't you fret. And when they were younguns they looked up and saw faces he had never seen that were still young then and dead and gone now long ago.

And so on back with them too. A way on back through the mountains. A way on back through the years. Took you deeper on back then you could ever study.

Now don't you fret.

He looked around the dark room, and down at his son, and back in to the wall. He shook his head once, very gravely.

Long ways.

Can't never get back.

Oh sure you can go back home. Good to go home and see the old folks.

All the places you used to know. The ones that stayed.

But if you ever leave it, so much grows up between you can't ever honestly get all the way back in your life.

And what's the good of it.

All I aimed to make of myself. Left my people and sweat blood to get.

What's the good.

All that happens, you don't get what you started after, and you can't ever get back where you started.

Thought I hated it. Couldn't get away soon enough to suit me.

I sure did find out different.

Just one way.

You make you a home of your own and you get you a youngun, boy of your own, even a girl. And ever so often there's something they do, makes you remember. Even just some way they look or you know how they feel.

Then all of sudden you know just exactly how it feels to be that young and ignorant. Look at the logs in a wall and don't even know they're logs or it's a wall.

Because you remember then.

How your folks felt to see you too, and you put them in mind of when they were younguns.

Because now you feel like they did then.

You even begin to know what it's going to feel like to get old. Have grandchildren.

Die.

You know what it feels like to be so little and funny you can't do for yourself and it's pretty near the same as if you were your own self again, as little and far aback as you can remember.

He looked down again at his son.[8]

Jay is very aware of a continuity from generation to generation, and of the similarities between city and country. He wants his son to have the advantages of city life, but he also does not want him to be separated from valuable country ties. Ohlin has pointed out that Rufus is "the last link of a long chain."[9] Through the father's interest that chain is unbroken. Jay instinctually appreciates his ties with family and the country. Those ties remain important.

A revealing interchange occurs during a Sunday outing to visit Jay's great-great-grandmother. On their way the parents attempt to determine the age of the grandmother, and Mary comments "'—why she's almost as old as the country, Jay.'" The comments, which follow, suggest much about each parent. Jay laughs:

> "Oh, no," . . . "Ain't nobody that old. Why I read somewhere, that just these mountains here are the old-est. . . ."
> "Dear, I meant the nation," she said. "The United States, I mean. Why let me see, why it was hardly as old as I am when she was born." They all calculated for a moment. "Not even as old," she said triumphantly.[10]

He is thinking of the physical world; but Mary in a structured manner thinks of the government. Dealing in abstract concepts is not Jay's usual mode of thought. During the trip to visit the grandmother Agee effectively contrasts the city and country ways of thinking about family and nature. Each of the parents' actions reveals themselves. The mother is eager to let Rufus meet his great-grandmother, but she is not sure exactly how much he should be allowed to experience. The reality of how hard life can be, and of approaching death, is disturbing. The father's attitude is different. When the old, old woman is kissed by Rufus, the child overhears "his mother's voice say, 'Jay,' almost whispering, but his father says, 'Let her be.'" He means, let Rufus learn.

Such differences in attitude between parents are a basic ingredient in the novel. When Rufus and Jay go to the movies, it is clear that they are in league, and that the mother does not really approve of enjoying Charlie Chaplin who goes around hooking up skirts with his cane. Such crudeness is simply uncalled for. Nor would Mary have approved of Rufus being taken into a saloon.

Significantly, when Jay leaves to visit his sick father, Mary begins thinking about the father-in-law whom she seems to feel did not possess the ambition which a more enterprising (perhaps urban?) person might possess.

> There was a special . . . weakness about him . . . which took advantage, and heaped disadvantage and burden on others and it was not even ashamed for itself, not even aware. . . . Jay's father was the one barrier between them, the one stubborn, unresolved, avoided thing, in their complete mutual understanding of Jay's people, his "background."[11]

What especially seems to disturb Mary as she thinks of her husband's father is the fact that he appeared to be resigned to his situation. Further, he was generous and never complained. Mary appears to feel that Jay's father might have been more aggressive and should have assumed more responsibility.

Jay seems to have manifested few of these passive traits. He was a strong person but must have also shared some characteristics with his father. On the day of the funeral when Walter Starr takes the children home, he compares Jay to Lincoln. Starr qualifies his thoughts about Jay in this way: "I don't mean getting ahead. I mean the right things. He wanted a good life, and good understanding, for himself, for everybody."[12] Significantly Jay's characterization demonstrated that the competitive demands of urban life make it more difficult to achieve the harmony which men should feel with each other and with nature.

A good example of this awareness is when Rufus is teased by neighborhood boys. Such regular teasing is possible when many boys are often together while their fathers go into town to work. (It would not be so possible on a mountain farm.) It is Jay who realizes that Rufus will have to learn how to confront such teasing. Even the visiting Uncle Ted enjoys teasing Rufus. Uncle Ted and Aunt Kate (significantly, they are the mother's relatives from Michigan) come for a visit, and Rufus is told that if he whistles hard enough the cheese will jump off the table. The uncle derives considerable fun from teasing the child, and subsequently Rufus's mother also gets angry with Jay because he does not intervene:

> "I don't care, Jay! . . . if you won't stand up for him, I will,
> I *can* promise you that."
> "It was just a joke," his father said.[13]

Uncle Ted protests that surely no one would really believe what he told Rufus, and Mary insists that the child's trust has been violated. Jay does his best to stop the arguing, but he realizes that Rufus will have to learn to cope with such problems. The implication is that Jay knows such arguing remains petty, as is much of what men do.

Jay, who manifests a deep respect for harmony in nature and with other persons, does not enjoy seeing others taken advantage of. Earlier on this same day, when adults were laughing at Catherine, the littlest member of the family, it was he who quietly remarked, "Doesn't anybody like to be laughed at." But it is also he who realizes that teasing and being teased can not be fully controlled. He knows that such small actions are especially insignificant when compared to the grandeur of nature. Jay's mountain background seems to make this apparent to him. It is significant that on an outing with Uncle Ted and Aunt Kate, an excursion trip up into the Smokey Mountains, it was Jay who took great pleasure in pointing out the mountains. Rufus remembered:

> the train took a long curve and . . . he heard his mother say, "*Ohhh*! How perfectly *glorious*!", and his father say shyly, a little as if he owned them and was giving them to her, "That's them. That's the Smokies all right."[14]

But Aunt Kate, who accompanies the family, is not impressed at all. When she is told to look at the mountains, she does so for only a second and then drifts off to sleep again. Jay knows what these mountains mean, and what kind of lives they have provided for men. He has affection for them. During the morning of the outing, when all the family was awaiting the train, everyone had enjoyed the flavor of the station. The picture of the L&N station is reported through the eyes of the child, Rufus.

> His mother told Uncle Ted she liked it better than the Southern depot because there were so many country folks and his father said he did too. It smelled like chewing tobacco and pee, and like a barn. Some of the ladies wore sunbonnets and lots of the men wore old straw hats, not the flat kind. One lady was nursing her baby.[15]

The reader realizes that the more urbanized mother and her northern relatives did not look upon the country people waiting in the station in just the same way as did Jay who knew firsthand a way of life. The smells and sensuousness of the waiting room might well have been considered vulgar by those who had not experienced the hardship and comfort of the deep country. Agee's novel often reminds its reader of the positive values associated with the rugged life of the Tennessee mountains.

Notes

[1] *Let Us Now Praise Famous Men* (Boston, 1941), p. 393.

[2] Charles W. Mayo, *James Agee: His Literary Life and Work* (unpublished doctoral dissertation, George Peabody College for Teachers, 1969), p. 26.

[3] "Working Notes" for *A Death in the Family*. The University of Texas Library. This material is gratefully used with the permission of the James Agee Trust.

[4] *The Collected Poems of James Agee* (Boston, 1968), p. 59.

[5] *A Death in the Family* (New York, 1967), p. 33.

[6] *Death*, p. 47.

[7] *Death*, p. 99.

[8] Variant manuscript for *A Death in the Family*. The University of Texas Library.

[9] Peter Ohlin, *Agee* (New York, 1966), p. 207.

[10] *Death*, p. 232.

[11] *Death*, p. 51.

[12] *Death*, p. 303.

[13] *Death*, pp. 245-246.

[14] *Death*, p. 243.

[15] *Death*, p. 242.

Religious Faith in *The Morning Watch**

Commentators on Agee's *The Morning Watch* (1951) emphasize the growth into maturity of its twelve year old hero, Richard. But Agee's focus remains more specifically upon the immediacy of what is experienced, and less on change than is usually assumed.[1] Agee's text, his working notes, excluded manuscript, and the biographical circumstances which contributed to the development of the novella all point toward an understanding of the book which recognizes the stasis which is the center of the work. This novella achieves success because of its focus upon a pinnacle of religious fervor which the reader senses must inevitably diminish. The book is about the hours of the Maundy Thursday vigil and morning of Good Friday when students at a rural boarding school are allowed to make visits before the exposed Blessed Sacrament in the Lady Chapel. Richard had been anticipating the vigil for months; he hoped to pray extremely well. Yet his hopes are not fulfilled, and the book is, in large part, a report of failure, while ironically he does experience genuine religious emotion. Throughout the hours portrayed Richard's mind is constantly distracted as he attempts to pray. After leaving the chapel, he and two other boys go for an early hour swim instead of reporting back to their dormitory. The swim, and other actions of Richard during the outing, are more distractions from his valiant effort to be religious. Nevertheless these hours include moments of high religious emotion; but hints that they inevitably pass are incorporated throughout the novella.

Throughout his fiction Agee was most interested in precisely focusing upon the intersections of space, time, and consciousness, and

---

* This article developes ideas outlined in my "James Agee's Unpublished Manuscript and His Emphasis on Religious Emotion in *The Morning Watch*," *Tennessee Studies in Literature* (1972), pp. 159-164.

less so in constructing plots and developing character. Because of that interest his best writing is often based on personal remembrance. In all of his longer works of fiction Agee's characters remain almost static while a kaleidoscopic world is beheld by them. Thus, six year old Rufus in *A Death in the Family* does not change within that novel, and it would be a mistake to expect development in his characterization. Essentially he beholds events which might influence later development. Basically the same thing occurs in *The Morning Watch*, even though more change might be expected with a six year older protagonist. *The Morning Watch* resembles Agee's *Let Us Now Praise Famous Men* where the writer concentrates upon particularities remembered, often complex states of mind. This semi-autobiographical novella recalls the atmosphere of St. Andrew's, the boarding school near Sewannee, Tennessee, remembered by Agee from childhood. Real persons are the basis of much of its characterization. In the working notes a list of remembered names parallels a list of characters.[2] One must assume that real events have had some bearing on the inception of this story.

Peter H. Ohlin, in *Agee* (New York: Obolensky, 1966, 188), has suggested that Richard's gradual change in awareness about suffering and death is the theme of the book. This element is important; but equally important is the almost static quality of these hours, and Richard's mood. The novella suggests how an intensely religious emotion is felt, and how such a feeling is intruded upon by other awarenesses. This is presented from the point of view of the artist looking back upon his own precocious childhood, a time during which a twelve-year old could hardly perceive the complexity of what he was experiencing.[3] Agee knew that religious emotion, for any person, was a combination of many different elements conjoined; but as one matures it becomes more difficult to reconcile religious feeling with other ways of feeling, thinking, and acting.

For Agee the late nineteen-forties had been a time of religious questioning. His 1948 and 1949 letters to Father Flye, who had been his teacher at St. Andrew's, reflect that thinking. Several times he noted his feelings were cyclical "between feeling relatively uninvolved religiously and very much" so. Sometimes he even felt a return to formal religion would be necessary, while at other times he was sure he would never return. But, along with these vacillations, he could say "at all times I feel sure that my own shapeless personal religious sense . . . is deepening and increasing."[4] Whether or not he might ever again have been a formal believer, his interest in religion remained important. One of his letters of this period says simply "I certainly feel no doubt to which side I am drawn 'as between Christ and those against Him'" (*Letters*, p. 175).

Another fact which contributed to Agee's religious awareness during the late nineteen-forties was his return to the campus of St. Andrew's during the early months of 1949. He had returned to his old school so that he could be present at the bedside of his dying stepfather. Spending some days on the campus where he had spent five years must have started his mind moving back imaginatively to a time when religious belief and ritual had been more important for him. His approach to the remembrance of that earlier time is similar to the remembrances of his "1928 Story." In that autobiographical story memory of an earlier more confident period provided the subject for a story which catches the complexity of a period when the young artist was confident about artistic abilities.[5] Agee, perhaps, remembered his earlier religious feelings in the same way.

Still another indication of an interest in religious matters preceding the composition of this novella is Agee's contribution as an "amateur" to a *Partisan Review* symposium "Religion and the Intellectuals" (February 1950). There he reiterated that he veered "between belief in God, nonbelief, and a kind of neutrality. In all three frames of mind I keep what I believe is meant by the religious consciousness" (112). Throughout his comments he stressed that religious belief, and conversion, is something ultimately inexplicable by rational means alone. "Certainly the final difficulties, for the intellectual only a little more so than for others, is that the crucial gap between religious belief and nonbelief cannot be closed—still less kept closed—rationally."

We know therefore that Agee had been seriously thinking about religious questions during the years immediately preceding his decision to write *The Morning Watch*. It is often mistakenly assumed that he worked on the manuscript for *The Morning Watch* over a period of several years. In fact, the book was written with one spurt of energy during the spring of 1950 (*Letters*, p. 181). Agee had spent "most of winter and spring" on his piece about John Huston. Then in a week the draft for the Maundy Thursday story was finished. The book is, therefore, the product of a period preceded by religious awareness; and a work which was written with relative speed. It seems to be an attempt artistically to recreate an earlier time of felt emotion.

The Morning Watch has been criticized because its ending is believed ineffective. Commentary often either expresses dissatisfaction with the lack of development in Richard's character, or explains his development in terms of the somewhat obvious symbolism incorporated into the work. Agee's emphasis, however, is upon the evocation of a particular fleeting moment; and attention to the particularities of what Richard sees and imagines is the primary means of evoking what he feels.[6] While what he experiences, both inside and outside the chapel does alter his consciousness, he feels at the end of his Good Friday's experience that he and his schoolmates remain "children."[7]

As he planned his book, Agee noted that the focus was to be on religious emotion, yet mixed with the "beginning of intrusions of [a] sense of beauty and a sense of science," while the general "watershed" about which the story was to flow was to remain the "age of faith at its height."[8] Essentially Richard's religious fervor is bounded by other experiences, and ultimately these hours will be lost. But during his watch the many forces at play within his mind are nearly balanced. Richard, of course, is not aware of all this. He is a rather bright boy who is attempting to feel religious.

Holy Weeks were special times for everyone at St. Andrew's. This time was so special that even Willard Rivenburg, the "great athlete" of St. Andrew's (who never even bothered to cross himself at crucial times in football games), was affected by the "stillness" which "came over everything" (21). For Richard the events of that week were the culmination of an elaborate series of attempts to foster religious emotion. His entire preceding year had been devoted to an intensification of religious fervor, and as this day arrives he is aleady near a high point of religious feeling. During the entire year preceding Holy Week Richard had, he thought, elaborately intensified his fervor. Denial and mortification had been practiced throughout that year, and even more so during the forty days of Lent. But just as his initial thoughts about the importance of his approaching watch are interrupted while he is still in bed, his attempt to cultivate religious emotion is doomed. As the narrative opens he lies awake waiting to be called by Father Whitman. He tries to meditate about Christ's Passion. But his attempts are broken by the happiness and blasphemy of other boys in the dormitory, and by his own mental distraction. Occasionally in prayer he had been able to imagine Christ crucified, but often, as is the case when he is walking out of the dormitory, the image he imagined "was very little different from a pious painting" (11).

The attempt to pray in the chapel is interrupted with this pattern of distraction. As Richard kneels he recalls the enormous lengths to which his self-imposed acts of mortification had been carried. As one recalls Joyce's Stephen Daedalus, it does not seem impossible for Richard to have gone much further than eating worms and near tasting his excrement (44). And indeed, he cannot. His self-imposed program of penance and mortification becomes confused with imaginary acts that he might perform, and then his mind runs riot. He imagines himself crucified—a Tennessee news item. A newspaper headline flashes to mind: "STRANGE RITES AT MOUNTAIN SCHOOL." And suddenly he sinks "his face into his hands and prays in despair. 'O God forgive me!'" (51). Later, when he returns to the chapel for another half-hour watch he does come close to the realization for which he has been striving. Agee's working notes indicate that Richard's prayer would "finally, break through to sincere if over emotional realization." When he opens his eyes "in quiet wonder," it then did seem "to him the very day. Not just a day in remembrance, but the day" (86). But when this height of emotion is felt, it is made clear it must diminish. Richard realizes that on this day Christ will not see the sun set, and then almost simultaneously, he notices the candles on the altar which seem "spearing, aspiring, among the dying flowers" (86). Then his realization of what Good Friday is, is lost, and an emotion vaguely unsettling, takes hold:

> Something troubled him which he had done or had left
> undone, some failure of the soul or default of the heart
> which he could not now quite remember or was it perhaps
> foresee; he was empty and idle, in some way he had failed.
> Yet he was also filled to overflowing with a reverent and
> marveling peace and thankfulness. My cup runneth over,
> something whispered within him, yet what he saw in his
> mind's eye was a dry Chalice, an empty Grail. (87)

This implication seems to be that only in years following will Richard realize that it was his imagination coupled with religious fervor (not religious emotion alone) which kindled the image of a "dry Chalice." With that image Agee hints at what is in store for Richard.

Throughout the novella Richard's attempts to pray lead him through a series of distractions. Indeed there is hardly a thought which does not lead him quickly astray. At the end of his first half-hour in the chapel he realizes that mostly "his mind had been wandering: there had been scarcely one moment of prayer or of realization" (61). Much of the book devoted to Richard's attempts to pray is a record of his distracted mental state. While these hours are a high point of religious emotion, they are ironically a constant series of deviations from the path Richard desperately wants to follow. For instance, he is hardly in the chapel when its atmosphere of candles and flowers, which should allow him to think of God, drives his mind to remembrances of his father's funeral. When he tries to pray "Soul of Christ sanctify me. . . . Blood of Christ inebriate me," his thoughts immediately flash to an interest in the derivation of the word "inebriate," and it is not long before he recalls "drinking sodapop in Knoxville [with] boys slightly more worldly than he [who] would twist the bottle deep into the mouth and cock it up vertically to drink. . . . 'Ahhh, good ole whiskey!'" (33). But this was not even whiskey, he thought. Blood. And then, all the sudden, he is recalling the blasphemous remarks which his uncle had made, "'There is a pudding filled with blood.'" Finally, Richard forces such thoughts out of his mind momentarily. But then the word "Wounds" does the same thing.

A similar pattern of distraction continues throughout his watch. Even when he realizes how he is distracted, and how that is sinful, he immediately sees how he was proud: in his recognition of pride "it began to occur to him that not many people would even know . . . the terrible sin it was" (78). Richard is balancing on a precarious ledge. When he recognizes his offense he immediately seeks to balance it with resolution "until it began to seem as if he were tempted into eternal wrong by rightness itself or even the mere desire for rightness and as if he were trapped between them, good and evil, as if they were mirrors laid face to face . . . (78-79).

Richard wants desperately to maintain what he assumes to be a proper religious frame of mind. But Agee stresses that religious fervor is being infringed upon by other awarenesses. The working notes and excluded manuscript written in conjunction with the novella support a reading which emphasizes the futility of the young protagonist's attempt to sustain his religious feeling as it is intruded upon by all manner of things from sex to skepticism. In his working notes Agee asked himself what he hoped to accomplish. And his answers, as well as unused introductory and concluding passages, indicate that he felt his story should imply that innocence would yield to other ways of experiencing the world. Agee asked himself the following:

> What really am I after in this story and is it worth doing? Religion at its deepest intensity or clarity of childhood faith and emotions; plus beginnings of a skeptical intellect and set of senses; how the senses themselves, and sexuality, feed the skeptical or non-religious or esthetic intellect; efforts at self-discipline. Religious-esthetic-biological experiences carrying with them above all, religious experience of an unusually fine kind, and the innocent certainty that it is doomed.

When for instance, Agee suggests Richard's attempts to feel religious are clouded by his remembrances of pious paintings, he implies that the young artist-to-be is distracted by the developing esthetic sense. The phrase "Within Thy wounds hide me," gives rise to a series of distractions, until finally "in his mind's eye, made all the worse by all the most insipid and effeminate, simpering faces of Jesus that he had ever seen in pictures, was this hideous image of a torn bleeding gulf at the supine crotch, into which an ant-swarm of the pious, millions of them . . . struggled to crowd themselves." Agee noted that he wanted to do the book in terms of:

> the watching in the chapel; wanderings of the mind and efforts at prayer; memories of the dead father; imaginations of sex and sport; workings of guilt; excesses of religious intention and complications of guilt and pride; the excitement of . . . dawn . . . the locust hull; . . . the snake.

But then he asked:

> Is [the snake] too obvious a symbol, and the locust? They seem so.
> Is this worth doing? I can't get any solid hold of it or confidence in it.
> A much gentler way of seeing and writing it? Or more casual? Mine is very dry and very literary.

These notes emphasize why there is little concern with characterization in the book. Agee wants to evoke "religious-esthetic-biological experiences." He even expresses doubt about his use of symbolism, the very element of the book most criticized. Richard Chase has argued that in place of "relaxed and perspicacious biography of spiritual change" the concluding parts of the book provide "spectacular semantic gestures."[9] There does seem to be excessive symbolism within the final pages of the book; but that part of the narrative is small, in quantity and import, in comparison with the dominant second part where Richard's attempts at prayer are basic. The chief concern in both the main middle part and the final section is an image of an intently religious child during hours which encompass the most solemn religious feast of the year.

Agee realized that perhaps too many elements in his narrative were too elaborately developed. In another of his working notes he suggested that he suspected "so many particularities. They drag, and they are dull. I keep working for the maximum number, an inch-by-inch account, when what I am after is the minimum in word and image, and a short handing of action." It must have been for such reasons he did rely upon the symbolism of the concluding section of the book. The shell which Richard finds, and with which he is fascinated, certainly connotes death and suffering. Yet Agee was doubtful about the effectiveness of that symbol. Its function in the narrative suggests a change in the boy's awareness about suffering; and his awareness will, importantly, provide a propensity for later development. But as the book closes Richard does not fully understand what the locust shell signifies, as he holds it "in exquisite protectiveness" (120).

Similarly, after he kills the snake (Satanic, but also Christlike) he realizes his hand is fouled from its killing. He vaguely senses an equation between his brave action and his religiosity:

> He looked coldly at his trembling hand: bloody at the knuckles and laced with slime, which seemed to itch and to burn as it dried, it still held the rock.
> "Better warsh that stuff off," Hobe said. "Git in your blood; *boy!*" . . . he began to feel that he had been brave in a way that he had never been brave before and he wanted the hand to clear gradually and naturally, the way the smudge clears from the forehead on Ash Wednesday. (111)

Richard senses all things fade. Yet he cannot fully realize that his religious emotion, which he has been desperately trying to enflame, will also fade. Almost immediately the boys go back to the school, and quickly as they are walking, Richard remembers with "surprise and shame" what day it is. He then continues thinking about the Passion.

Several crucial events occur to Richard in this last episode of the book. These experiences prepare him for later and inevitable change, but he does not mature during these few hours. More is expected of Richard than Agee ever hoped to handle, or could handle in a work of this scope, if we expected Richard to exhibit maturation. During these hours he is beginning to doubt the efficacy of formal religious practices. The novella concentrates on just the "beginnings of a skeptical intellect and set of senses."

Religiosity, yet simultaneously intense emotion, supports Richard's actions throughout the book. After he leaves the Lady Chapel the physical experiences become more important, but the effect of the change is seldom something about which he is fully aware. The air outside the chapel is "so different from the striving candles and the expiring flowers that the boys were stopped flatfooted on the gravel" (91); but Richard also continues to remind himself that it is Good Friday.

When F. W. Dupee initially reviewed the novella he noted that the final scene at the Sand Cut was "not so well conceived" as the section set in the chapel, and he wondered if the "triumph in the chapel is not being capitalized on to an extent that is hardly legitimate."[10] What should be emphasized is that the focus of the novella remains, even during the forbidden swim, on Richard's religious fervor. In that climactic scene, the dive and the attempt to stay under water an extremely long time is certainly an act of pride and a crucial step toward maturation; but it is also an act of religious devotion. The dive is symbolic of a rebirth after his failure to sustain the kind of emotion that he hoped for in the chapel. But Richard, as he dives, has "just time to dedicate within himself *for Thee!*," and his dive becomes an act of devotion. He prays "O Lord let me suffer with Thee this day," as his lungs are about to burst (104). It is as if the religious emotion itself is near bursting. But it is important that the emotion does not collapse. Richard is still able, a moment later, to stand on the bank of the quarry and imagine what Jesus had suffered at that very moment.

The concluding section remains fundamentally built on the

boy's intently religious attitudes during hours which remain very much part of a religious feast. However, Agee's fear that his method of writing was perhaps elaborate and too "literary" provides an insight into what he did accomplish—a sense of immediacy, and evocation of emotion, but emotion almost ready to disintegrate. In a related note he had written "R's waking emotion and the hollowness of the dormitory beds must be as nearly immediate and simultaneous as possible." Any indirection, abstraction, or use of symbols, unless very carefully integrated into the experience as a whole, would tend to detract from the immediacy of that moment.

No doubt Agee experienced difficulty deciding how the emphasis upon Richard's emotion would be best focused. There are several draft versions for alternate openings for the book. And, in addition, an introductory section and alternate ending were actually typed out. Whether these alternate passages were submitted to an editor is unknown; but it is clear that Agee was not sure how best to begin the novella.

The introductory manuscript is also about the difficulty of feeling religious emotion, but from the point of view of an adult. In the excluded passage Father Whitman, a priest who wakes the boys from their chapel visit, tries to feel, but cannot, the solemnity of the night. For him the meaning of the Passion is clear intellectually, but it is not something which he can feel. His disturbed thoughts provide insight into Richard's dilemma:

> however clearly he realized it in his dull, tired mind, he could not realize it in his heart. He remembered how the mother of one of the boys on the place, a widow who lived just off the grounds, had spoken once of that kind of reward, as rare, but wonderful, and compensating for all, and to be relied on, and how he had told her that in twenty years of hoping, it had never once happened to him. I only want to be a religious, he told himself quietly. I haven't got it in me to be, and in twenty years of trying, none of that has changed.

Then Father Whitman's mind is distracted by his pocketwatch, and the excluded opening concludes:

> When at last the watch marked sixteen minutes of four, he briefly and formulatically completed his prayers, made the

> long firm sign of the cross which usually for a little while
> deeply confirmed him in his faithfulness, shut off the
> alarm, got up from the cot, and went as silently as he could
> down the corridor into Number Twelve to wake three
> more boys.[11]

The implication of Richard's incipient awareness, qualified by the opening description of Father Whitman, is that with maturity, religious emotion is complicated, and easily distracted. Throughout the novella Richard is not particularly aware of how his religious fervor functions. He cannot yet understand that religious emotion will not be forced.[12] In the excluded passage the dull emotion of Father Whitman stands in contrast with the "sincerely devout" feelings of Richard.[13] Father Whitman who has been a religious for twenty years, tries to meditate. He lies awake waiting to call the boys to their watch, but he realizes that Maundy Thursday and Good Friday have lost any special aura for him.

In conjunction with the unused introductory passage Agee's "possible addition" for the conclusion would also have slightly altered the book's emphasis. Agee suggested if the alternate opening was employed lines would "be added onto present ending, no new paragraph." These words were added to the working draft as well as typed in conjunction with the alternate opening for the work. On the last page of the narrative Richard approaches the school dormitory with his errant friends; he is carrying the locust shell which he had picked up in the woods, "his left hand sustaining, in exquisite protectiveness, the bodiless shell which rested against his heart" (120). The excluded ending added these phrases: ". . . and exactly as he had foreseen, there on the back steps was Father Whitman, and although his eyes too were just as Richard had foreseen, hard, sleepless, patient, eyes to be afraid of and ashamed before, it was not so very hard to meet them after all."

With a beginning which suggests the difficulty of sustaining religious fervor, and a conclusion which again returns to Father Whitman, the emphasis upon an "age of faith at its height," would have been more clearly evident. Throughout *The Morning Watch* Agee is most concerned with evoking the complex emotion of particular imagined moments, the high point in Richard's life. Agee is fascinated with the beauty of that time. The beauty is mostly in the immediacy, Richard is not aware of the vast differences between what he has attempted to experience and what actually has happened. Such a realization can only be made by a wiser person: Father Whitman or Agee, the artist, as he fictionalizes these moments.

Notes

[1] William J. Rewak, S.J., "James Agee's *The Morning Watch*: Through Darkness to Light" *The Texas Quarterly*, 16 (Autumn 1973), pp. 21-37, for instance, insists that Agee's "one major concern [is] the growth into maturity of the young hero," p. 22.

[2] Working notes, autograph manuscript, *The Morning Watch*, University of Texas Library. Other manuscript material demonstrates that Agee based his book on specific recollections of St. Andrew's. The cottage in which his mother lived near the school (which still exists on the west side of the campus) is, interestingly, in an opposite direction from the Sand Cut of Part III. Richard's flight, therefore, was both a movement away from the chapel and campus, and from his mother with whom he associated religious ideas. One excluded fragment develops Richard's interest in "the Christian year," and there he associates the idea of being an exile with his mother's insistence that he not visit the cottage except during official holidays such as Christmas. This material and all additional material from the Agee Papers at Texas is gratefully used with the permission of the James Agee Trust.

[3] Charles W. Mayo in his unpublished dissertation (Peabody, 1969), p. 234, documents Agee's approval of a review of *The Morning Watch* by Robert Phelps which suggests the story deals with "the abrasively self-conscious sensibility usually identified with an artist as a young man." ("Texture of Life," *Freeman*, I [August 27, 1951)], p. 767.)

[4] James Agee, *The Letters of James Agee to Father Flye* (New York: George Braziller, 1962), p. 184.

[5] "1928 Story" is part of my "Agee in the Forties: Unpublished Poetry and Fiction," *Texas Quarterly*, 11 No. 1 (1968), pp. 23-37.

[6] Ohlin rightly demonstrates how the emphasis within the chapel is upon "the static nature of the scene" (*Agee*, p. 186).

[7] *The Morning Watch* (Boston: Houghton Mifflin, 1951), p. 119. Subsequent references to the text are noted parenthetically.

[8] *The Morning Watch*: pages of incomplete drafts (on sheet headed "notes") n.d. University of Texas Library.

[9] "Sense and Sensibility." *The Kenyon Review*, 13 (Autumn 1951), p. 691.

[10] F. W. Dupee, "Pride of Maturity." *The Nation*, February 28, 1951, p. 401. One

should also realize that there are strong "scenic parallels," as well as thematic ones, between the chapel and the Sand Cut episodes. J. Douglas Perry, in his unpublished dissertation (Temple University, 1968) elaborates this point. See especially p. 209.

[11] *The Morning Watch*: note, typed and typed carbon copy with autograph emendation (3 pp.), n.d., University of Texas Library. The entire fragment is edited in the *Tennessee Studies* article, pp. 162-164.

[12] See Ohlin, *Agee*, p. 190; and John S. Philipson "Character, Theme, and Symbol in *The Morning Watch*," *Western Humanities Review*, XV (Autumn 1961), p. 367, for development of this ironic point.

[13] Working notes, *op. cit.*

V

Making an Autobiographical Novel

Projecting a Story

Putting together a final composite manuscript for James Agee's posthumous novel *A Death in the Family* (New York: McDowell, Obolensky, 1957) was a difficult editorial task. Agee died before completing the final revisions for the novel, although he felt only a few months of writing remained. His manuscript, a pencil holograph which is difficult to read because of the minuteness of its script, includes variant material which falls outside the principal narrative, and Agee had not decided how he could best incorporate all of that incomplete material. His editors chose to use a large portion of this unplaced material within the composite novel and to indicate the unfinished state with italics. But instead of arbitrarily fitting those italicized sections within the text, before or after the narrative they decided to place the italicized passages between the natural divisions of the narrative—before Part I (the death); Part II (the evening of the death); and Part III (the day of the funeral). How those italicized sections could have been placed differently has been a subject of discussion by critics of the novel.[1]

It appears that the sequential chapters of the book which describe the death and the days surrounding it, chapters 1-20, were virtually complete at his death, and perhaps even had been arranged as a finished unit by him.[2] But the non-sequential material, most of which is incorporated into the italicized sections of the novel (though some remains unpublished), was considerably less organized. From the working notes for the novel it appears that Agee must have been planning a much longer autobiographical work, and the sequential narrative as published would probably finally have formed only the concluding portion of a projected longer novel.

Some twenty pages of working notes accompany the manuscript and indicate Agee was planning an extensive autobiographical recollection of his childhood. The following excerpt is typical of many notes he jotted, and indicative of a larger plan. This partial transcription constitutes one outline for which there are several variants. Only a few of the episodes noted here were actually written and now form a part of *A Death in the Family*. But it is important to observe that the last sentence, in fact, summarizes the sequential narrative from chapter 1 through the final chapter of the published book. Agee wrote:

> Open at night
> Next morning (Friday) : breakfast: a weekday:
> return in evening. Saturday. Chilhowee Park?
> .... Sunday: ice cream freeze. Chicken killing.
> Either they come up to us or we go down to them.
> Either way, get in new characters.
>
> Holiday & Trips
> 4th of July. Labor Day (hardly observed). Halloween.
> Thanksgiving. Birthday. Christmas. New Years.
> Easter. They go out to a party or wedding. Trip
> by train to La Follette. Trip to Elkmont.
>
> The car. dialogue as written. Enter the Ford.
> General writing on trips. Looking for a country
> place. Topside. Trip or trips to Grandparents.
>
> Autumn trip. Cider, ripe apples, hogs, Sunday
> afternoon. When and where, the stuff at the corner?
> Then he takes me to the movies: and soon, to end
> of book.[3]

This sketch seems to represent the writer's awareness of many possibilities for autobiographical remembrance. Additional related outline sketches provide still other listings of episodes and remembrances. Sometimes Agee began such listings with the phrase "Lead as now," which possibly means that the book could have been arranged to begin in the present and to move imaginatively back toward the earlier times as remembered.[4] The novel as outlined, and as it stands in its composite form, is certainly based on remembrances from childhood, and possesses only a minimum of plot. The following notes which occur on the same page as the outline transcribed above suggest Agee's hopes for his work:

> Maximum simple: Just the story of my relation with my
> father, and, through that, as thorough as possible an image

of him: winding into other things on the way but never
dwelling on them. Open at night. Then the sense impressions beginning with my mother; back to him. Long & short
all jumbled together? no special clear sense of time? any
cutback through which his story is told? equal play between his and mine?[5]

The main thing he seems to have wanted to accomplish was simply to
relate the remembrance of his relation with his father; but this could
be done by "winding into other things on the way." Had the larger plan
developed into an extended work there evidently could have been
considerably more attention devoted to memories of childhood, family
meetings, and pleasures, before the death is sketched in the outline
notes.

In further working notes Agee suggested how the problems of
marriage, friction between the parents, and questions about how best
the children were to be raised, disciplined, and educated might be
incorporated into a longer work. Thus as he wrote the manuscript for
A Death in the Family he seems to have realized that he might write a
much more elaborate and detailed autobiographical fictionalized
remembrance. Some of the variant material which accompanies the
manuscript for *A Death in the Family* seems to be related to that larger
projected work.

Apparently Agee began an autobiographical novel many different times. Several fragments, which may have been intended as
openings for a book, are in existence. However, the editors chose the
earlier, and perhaps more harmonious "Knoxville: Summer of 1915" as
an introductory passage. Its mood is similar to many parts of the book,
but it had already been published and has only an indirect connection
with the novel through the mood it evokes, and there is no indication
within the manuscript or notes that Agee would have included it.
"Knoxville: Summer of 1915" was aleady published ten years before
the book proper was begun.[6]

Related rejected manuscript materials provide additional insight into what Agee sought to accomplish with this novel. For
instance, the fragment "Now as awareness" which Robert Fitzgerald
included in *The Collected Short Prose of James Agee* is important because
it clarifies some of Agee's motivation behind the composition of *A
Death in the Family*. This fragment employs imagery similar to many
effective sections within the novel. In "Now as awareness" Agee

suggests that he will rely upon "bald narration," but his statement of intent is presented in rhetorical and poetic language. He remarks that he wanted to remember all those persons

> who have gone before, backward beyond remembrance and beyond the beginning of imagination, backward among the emergent beasts, and the blind, prescient ravenings of the youngest sea, those children of the sun, I mean, who brought forth those, who wove, spread the human net, and who brought forth me; they are fallen backward into their graves like blown wheat and are folded under the earth like babies in blankets, and they are melted upon the mute enduring earth like leaves.[7]

Such a sense of wonder informed him as he began to reconstruct the world of his remembered childhood, a remembrance which is at the core of *A Death in the Family*. His attempts at "bald narration" provided him with an open-ended method to write about his earliest memories; the result is a book "classed as fiction but largely factual from his childhood and family."[8] It appears that it would have been possible to include many more episodes.

It is often assumed that Agee's novel was virtually complete before he died; and the editorial note which has been provided for its many editions supports such an assumption. But the unused manuscript materials and working notes which accompany the book demonstrate that while the text, as edited, represents a final stage of writing, it seems to be of a shorter version. It is a matter of conjecture to suggest what Agee might have later developed. But his editors were confronted by many decisions in establishing a final text for the sections included in the unfinished novel. Typographical errors and misreadings of Agee's minute penciled script were introduced into the book by them; and because variant words and phrases appear in the manuscript, they had to make choices about which words would be most appropriate for a published text.[9] Still more questions arise from the accompanying excluded manuscript material.

The editorial note which accompanies *A Death in the Family* states that "nothing has been eliminated except for a few cases of first-draft material which [Agee] later reworked at greater length, and one section of seven-odd pages which the editors were unable satisfactorily to fit into the body of the novel."[10] Examination of the manuscript materials, however, reveals that this statement is misleading. Most

importantly, a section that can be designated "Dream Sequence" perhaps written as an introduction for the book, has been ignored.[11] That
dream, a nightmare in which the narrator (Agee?) returns to the scene
of his childhood, establishes a mood considerably different from that
of "Knoxville: Summer of 1915," the 1938 sketch which was chosen as
an appropriate opening for the novel. The "Dream Sequence" runs to
nine pages in Agee's tight script.[12] (Two other fragments edited for the
Collected Short Prose, "Run Over" and "Give Him Air," are similar in
both theme and style to "Dream Sequence."[13] Both of those pieces
report an accident and describe a victim badly mangled and dying. In
mood they resemble "Dream Sequence" but the suggestion of dream-
ing is absent. Both seem reports of fact. The first of these is about the
death of a cat—given in the most horrible detail. It ends with the
parenthetical statement: "Things like this are happening somewhere
on the earth every second." The second report is about a man killed in
an automobile accident. The "Dream Sequence" contains some of the
same horror as these two fragments.) The sequence has a completely
different tone from "Knoxville: Summer of 1915"; if it had even been
used as an introduction for the book, the tone of the remembrance as
evoking a whole world would have been altered. Both passages raise
similar questions about identity and the mystery of being a person. In
the sketch about the summer of 1915 Agee emphasizes the comfort
which the child felt in the presence of his family. In "Dream Sequence"
he emphasizes that moments from earlier experience retain a distinct
beauty which can be evoked by the artist, and when such evocation
is successful, meaning is projected into the chaos and mystery of
living.

"Dream Sequence" is based on personal remembrance, but
images of childhood are fused in it with the horror of contemporary
times which seem nightmarish. In its near surrealistic method, this
dream differs from most of Agee's writing. It resembles Céline, a
writer he read and admired.[14] The way a scene can suddenly shift from
broiling heat to freezing cold or the maddening way people on a street
can ignore the horrible is reminiscent of *Journey to the End of the Night*.
And, as "Dream Sequence" is read it becomes clearer and clearer that
the only action which has any meaning for the narrator is an act of
artistic integrity. Essentially this dream takes place in an urban setting
and is an account of the narrator's attempt to provide burial for a
victim of mob violence. In the course of the dream it becomes clear that

the victim is the narrator's father. Elements from the present are connected with ideas and facts from earliest childhood. The death, the absence, and the "betrayal" of the father all seem to be related to the disappointments of the dreamer with his contemporary world. But it is impossible to understand how past and present are related. What is significant is that after the nightmare has been suffered it is clear to the dreamer that he must "go back" into the years of his childhood—exactly what Agee does in *A Death in the Family*. When that "journey" is accomplished and performed with honesty, some peace of mind can be found, even though the chaos of the contemporary world remains. Agee apparently realized (as he was writing the novel) that it was much more important for him to perform the individual artistic act, "a simple act of veneration," than it was to remain worried about problems of contemporary society.[15] In the "Dream Sequence" the explicit point is made that something like the clarity of earlier times can be achieved by artistic means. Even if the present is horrible and there are few answers about what it means to be a person, that which is carefully delineated with words has a value of its own. Words can evoke the emotion and comfort of earlier experiences.

As Agee was planning *A Death in the Family*, it appears that he wanted to employ a technique similar to that which he had already employed in *Let Us Now Praise Famous Men*. That is, he would write about only what he could remember. That plan apparently broadened after the novel was begun—yet it is significant that many of the most successful passages of the book remain based on personal remembrance. Look at the opening and closing sections of the book (chapters 1, 2, 19, and 20, and the inter-chapter material). The narrator of "Dream Sequence" suggests the writer's focus would be limited only to what he could recall:

> He thought of all he could remember about his father and about his own direct relations with him. He could see nothing which even faintly illuminated his darkness, nor did he expect ever to see anything, yet if he could be sure of anythng except betrayal and horror, he could be sure that that was where the dream indicated that he should go. He should go back into those years. As far as he could remember; and everything he could remember; nothing he had learned or done since; nothing except (so well as he could remember) what his father had been as he had known him, and what he had been as he had known him-

self, and what he had seen with his own eyes, and sup-
posed with his own mind.[16]

Such a statement suggests why Agee worked so conscientiously on
episodes which have little connection with each other except the
viewpoint of the child. Those episodes often appear to have been
constructed out of fragments remembered from childhood. In a related note he has written, after listing several possible episodes from
Rufus's point of view, "No, these things wd be unconnected in his
experience & so here."[17]

With evidence from both notes and the "Dream Sequence," it
seems that in an important sense Agee's book was closer to being
finished than otherwise might be suspected. It appears that, at least as
he once conceived it, this was not to be a novel in the sense of an
organic unit with all of the episodes woven into each other. He wanted
to write an account of his relationship with his father. His memory of
that relationship was fragmented; and for that reason it appeared that
the presentation as well might be fragmented. The re-creation of a
portion of his childhood was as close to an answer as he could hope for
concerning the meaning of his relationship with his father:

> Nothing he could hope to understand out of [the dream]
> was not already obvious to him. All the same, he could
> make the journey, as he had dreamed the dream, for its
> own sake without trying to interpret; and if the journey
> was made with sufficient courage and care, very likely that
> of itself would be as near the answer as he would ever hope
> to get.[18]

Going back into the years of childhood would provide a pleasure
similar to that which Jay and Rufus had enjoyed as they sat at a corner
on evenings after they had been to the movies together. Within the
"Dream Sequence" the corner to which the speaker must drag the body
of the victim is the same corner which appears in the first chapter of
the printed novel. The same outcropping of limestone, "like a great
bundle of dirty laundry," appears in both.[19] The same street is followed
by the dreamer as is followed by Jay and Rufus on their way home. The
alternate rejected manuscript section, which begins in nightmare but
ends in peacefulness, is therefore a symbolic account of Agee's realization that he had to ignore many of the horrors of the contemporary

world—even some of the confusion of his own life. If one stops trying to make sense of the world and instead responds to its mystery, then it becomes possible to celebrate existence.

The existence of "Dream Sequence" emphasizes that the book was a journey backward into the memories of childhood. Many of the incidents within the book, and within the unused manuscript material, seem to have a basis in fact. Especially this is the case with the materials which surround the death itself. In this regard some of the most interesting notes accompanying the manuscript are those on three closely written pages where Agee recorded what he could remember (or infer) about the day of his father's funeral. Many of those remembered details are significant because they are later found woven into the actual composition of the novel. Here are three short passages from these notes:

> As I remember it we were brought in first to see him alone, & unmolested. Then I think but am not sure, that I sneaked back in. Then if I remember rightly we are formally brought in once more, by Mother and Aunt Jessie and perhaps . . . with Father Robertson, and I realized faintly that he was the boss of this occasion, and obscurely resented his bossiness and intrusion, his sureness of the right to be there. . . .

> . . . I do remember our going past, and seeing him, quite briefly again. Very different in this context. I was most appalled by & interested in the strength of the odor of the flowers, & all their scarves and ribbons, and the feeling that everybody was looking at us. . . .

> But mainly I remember his [uncle's] needing (?) to tell me about the butterfly. "If I ever believe in God, it will be because I remember what I saw today. . . ."

> I don't know what magnificent means but through the word and the way he says it I am filled with a mysterious sense of glory.[20]

It is evident that all of that material has been incorporated into the novel. A consideration of even only the last of those passages illustrates how Agee took memories, and then used them to evoke the feelings of the fictional Rufus. Rufus cannot understand the meaning of the words which his uncle speaks—but he knows that something unusual has happened: the child was filled with a "sense of glory." In the climactic final chapter of the novel Agee reconstructed an artistic presentation of that earlier mysterious feeling. Rufus cannot understand the words his uncle uses:

> Miraculous, Magnificent. He was sure he had better not ask what they were. He saw a giant butterfly, and how he moved his wings so quietly and grandly. . . . Maybe "miraculous" was the way the colors were streaks and spots. . . . He could see it very clearly, because his uncle saw it so clearly when he told about it, and what he saw made him feel that a special and good thing was happening. He felt that it was good for his father and that lying there in the darkness did not matter so much. He did not know what this good thing was, but because his uncle felt that it was good, and felt so strongly about it, it must be even more of a good thing than he himself could comprehend.[21]

This passage is a reaction to the earlier one which suggests Rufus's emotions. Agee suggests the child's feeling by means of careful reiteration of the simple fact that Rufus could not understand what was happening. Yet it was not important for him to understand. So much else contributed to his complex feeling at that moment. Many of the lyrical passages in the novel appear to have evolved from similar specific remembrances of isolated childhood events.

Perhaps Agee would never have been able to finish a work like the one he projected, which would have incorporated more separate remembered events. The book, as we have it in its composite form, contains most of the elements within the following sketch written as part of the working notes. Here, in a listing of technical problems, he indicated that he was not certain how all the parts might fit. He underscored the word *Detachedly* before he provided the following outline:

> I had better figure out a good deal more about a short version, but I suspect in the long run I had better stop worrying about length or even form.
> Detachedly:
> A soft and somewhat precocious child. A middle-class religious mother. A father of country background. Two sets of relatives: hers middle class, northern born, more or less cultivated; his, of the deep mountain country.
> Begin with the complete security and the simple

pleasures and sensations.

Develop: the deficiency in the child which puts them at odds: the increasing need of the child for the father's approval.

Interrupt with the father's sudden death. Here either the whole family is involed, or it is told in terms of the child.

At end: the child is in a sense & degree doomed, to religion & to the middle class. The mother: to religiosity. New strains develop, or are hinted between her & her family.[22]

There could have been many ways other than the one chosen editorially for *A Death in the Family* of expanding such an outline. Certainly, the excluded manuscript fragments indicate Agee was seeking just such an expansion. Inclusion of more of the variant manuscript as part of the composite novel would have provided the reader with additional insight into the remembered family and Rufus's childhood, items finally as important to Agee's remembrance of his father and childhood as the days immediately surrounding the death.

Most of the variant manuscript which has been excluded from the novel deals with Rufus's earliest years and the atmosphere which surrounded him in his relationships with his family. For instance, there are at least five unused manuscript pages which are a development of the "simple pleasures and sensations." This material is often incomplete, like a sketch for later development; yet some of it is clearly written. Here for instance, is a self-contained episode:

Sometimes daddy leaned over and spit into the fireplace. When there was a fire it made a fine strong noise.

Once he leaned over and spit there and his mamma said why Rufus! and then much more seriously, Jay!

Daddy turned dark red.

A fine example, she said.

Then he looked mad as if he would say something but he didn't say anything.

I'm sorry Jay but really! she said after a minute.

Just let up on it Laura, he said.

I just meant I was sorry I embarrassed you dear, I mean specially in front of: her voice trailed off and she nodded toward him.

All right, Don't be sorry, I deserved it. But just let it go will you?

Of course Jay, she said very quietly. After that the air between them was stiff and they stayed quiet. Then after a

> while daddy looked at her and said I am sorry Laura. So am
> I dear, she said, and they both smiled warmly.
>   It was then that he realized that daddy never did it
> except when they were alone. So he took care that they
> were alone the next time he did it and his daddy let out the
> most surprising laugh and suddenly mussed up his hair
> but, still smiling, shook his head and said uh'uh. Your
> mama's right, he said. You musn't do that. Me neither.
>   It's all right up in the country, he said. But in town
> people don't like it and we live in town.
>   He said me neither but sometimes he still did it all the
> same.
>   But only if they were by themselves. Hard to teach an
> old dog new tricks, he said.

The presence of such manuscript material suggests what kind of episodes Agee might have developed at greater length. Such short episodes could have been elaborated and lengthened, and each episode would have served as an angle of Rufus's point of view. It would not have been necessary that these different episodes be woven completely together: placed in juxtaposition they could have much the same effect as one of Whitman's catalogs, a series of journal entries, or the diverse approaches of *Let Us Now Praise Famous Men*. Therefore a paragraph about the remembrance of how a piano sounded and felt, or a page about the furnishings in the grandparents' house, both of which exist in manuscript, could have been considered an integral part of this "novel." No doubt editors excluded them because they are short, or fragmentary, or disconnected. Whether Agee would have made such a decision remains impossible to say. His many interests, the manifold styles of *Let Us Now Praise Famous Men*, his constant experimentation, and the notes for this novel suggest he may not have felt a need for a completely unified approach. It might not have been necessary to fit all of the parts together.

One of the sections which appears to have been most interesting to Agee deals with the earliest memories of Rufus. There are several variants for this material and some of it is incorporated in the book, but some of the excluded manuscript is more detailed than what was printed. For instance, nothing just like the following appears in the book. These notes from the working draft suggest a time when Rufus was very small:

> The one with the deep voice was Daddy. Smoke
> came out of his nose.
> The one with the gentle voice was mama.
> Sometimes daddy held him way up to the top
> of the room and laughed. Mama was the one who
> washed him with slippery soap.

Several different attempts to write in this manner are preserved in the excluded manuscript. The presence of such variant material is indicative that Agee may have been contemplating a longer and more detailed version.

The same possibility exists with the more detailed variants excluded from the composite manuscript for the first section of the first interstice. Those parts which describe Jay's singing to Rufus represent a remembrance which must have intrigued Agee. Several pages of variant material exist for this section; and manuscript which was finally chosen for inclusion in the book seems to be an earlier and less-detailed version. A more complete picture of Jay would have been provided if the more-detailed—and probably later—version had been used. Some representative parallel passages from the novel and manuscript illustrate the difference. Agee's method is an elaborately poetic one, even going so far as to paraphrase Psalm 23 and to place that paraphrase in the mind of Rufus. But Agee attempted an imaginative treatment of Jay's background too. Of the two drafts, the printed version appears tighter and more lyrical, but the excluded variant seems more complete. Here are the opening passages of, first, the novel, and secondly, the rejected variant:

> Waking in darkness, he saw the window. Curtains, a
> tall, cloven wave, towered almost to the floor. Transparent,
> manifold, scalloped along their inward edges like the
> valves of a sea creature, they moved delectably on the air
> of the open window.

> He woke in darkness and knew only that he was wide
> awake and that he was breathing, then leaning his head to
> his left, he saw the window. Curtains towered almost from
> the floor to the ceiling tall and cloven. Transparent, mani-
> fold, waving along their inward edges like the valves of a
> sea creature they moved on the air of the open window like
> breathing.[23]

The rejected variant seems to be essentially an expansion of the earlier version. Similar differences are apparent throughout the two versions of the chapter. Rather than citing differences, however, it seems most significant to note that Agee himself was not pleased with the chapter. He wrote:

> I must decide between a completely detached and deeply subjective treatment. I doubt if in complete detachment there is a story there.
> Rather, do the subjective, as detachedly as possible. Cut the crap about the child of darkness.[24]

The kind of poetry which is contained in the printed version of this "darkness" section is not the "detached" style that Agree sought. Had he made the final choice about inclusion of manuscript he might have excluded the "darkness" chapter altogether. But the revised version seems closest to his desires, and it appears it should have been the version incorporated into the book. He wanted "the subjective, as detachedly as possible." This entire chapter could be expanded and re-edited. Especially this is the case concerning the last several pages of the chapter when Jay is alone, and muses about his background and present family situation. Agee wrote several different versions for this ending. It is, of course, debatable which is the most appropriate; but an important fact is that the unused manuscript appears to be both more complete and more detached.

Still other short sections of manuscript are problematic because of their brevity. The typescript page "A Birthday" reprinted in *The Collected Short Prose* is similar in method and content to other unpublished variant manuscript.[25] It is basically a record of one remembered moment, the combination of Thanksgiving and the child's fourth birthday. The drinking of sherry, urgings by the relatives for Rufus to speak a certain way, and the gift of a tiny toy swan make up this glimpse of childhood. Additional variant manuscript pages record memories about the grandparents' home, most especially the many different furnishings within the house. (Some of this material is little more than notes.) Rufus used to enjoy fingering the piano and looking at the paintings hung there:

> In the corner was a picture with lions. It was dark and the lions padded along in the moonbeams. . . .

In another picture it was dark and there was a big stone lion with a face kind of like Uncle Hugh, not a lion face but a man. In between his paws there were people sleeping. A man and a lady and a little baby and a donkey, and they had a little fire.

That was Jesus when he was a little baby and his mama and his foss, *Foss.*

Foss-tur-father Rufus. . . .[26]

It would have been impossible to fit all of these fragments into any coherent whole, and Agee's editors justifiably wanted to put a book together which had a cohesiveness. For probably just such reasons the section "Surprise" was excluded from the composite manuscript.[27] This excluded section is carefully written and could stand as a separate short story; but it could not have been printed as part of the composite novel had the chapter about Victoria remained. That italicized chapter introduces Victoria before Rufus visits his grandparents. In the "Surprise" chapter Rufus meets Victoria when he returns home. He even mistakenly assumes she might be the surprise. In choosing manuscript for the composite novel, naturally a criterion that had to be employed would be conflict with other parts of the book; accordingly, both of these passages could not be included.

Other sections of the manuscript material stand as separate episodes, clearly written and in a nearly finished state. Why, for instance, several beautiful paragraphs about the family cat were omitted from the composite manuscript is uncertain. Only their brevity really justifies exclusion. Perhaps that two-page section of manuscript was overlooked in the preparation of the composite manuscript. The paragraphs of a few hundred words center around the death of Oliver, the grandparents' big old cat. Whether or not this passage has a basis in fact is unknown, but it fits well with all the other parts of the fictional account. The independence of the cat, the attitudes of many different family members, and the meaning of death within the family and for the child are all handled in the short passage.

At least one additional large manuscript bloc did not find its way, in any form, into the book. That five-page section in Agee's small script is primarily a conversation between Jay and Laura, the parents. It deals with the question of their buying an automobile.[28] This excluded section is a chapter which might be labeled "Premonition."

It might even be the section labeled "dialogue as written" included in Agee's outline. Its exclusion may have occurred because the passage does not include, as do other italicized materials, at least some material from the point of view of Rufus. However, it would have been an appropriate piece of manuscript for inclusion, especially if still other sections which take place earlier within the chronological development of the family's history had not been excluded.[29] Just like the short section which describes the death of Oliver, the grandparents' cat, or like sections about sense impressions of playing with the piano, this dialogue provides still another remembrance about the family. Within the dialogue between Jay and his wife, threads are added to a pattern about religious faith, their love for one another, the other family members, and fear about the automobile. Agee wrote in his "working notes" that Jay was a "victim of progress." This excluded manuscript supports this assertion.

Agee's book was still in progress when he died, and it is evident that it was still growing. Passages such as the dialogue between the parents concerning the automobile and "Dream Sequence" should be included, at least as an appendix, in any new edition of *A Death in the Family*. Knowledge of other facets and dimensions of this chronicle still in process will help readers appreciate the composite novel more. Agee may never have finished the book as projected, but he would have kept on trying.

Notes

[1] Peter Ohlin, *Agee* (New York: Obolensky, 1966), pp. 194-195; J. Douglas Perry, "James Agee and the American Romantic Tradition" (Ph.D. dissertation, Temple University, 1968), pp. 225-240.

[2] When I interviewed him at Monteagle, Tennessee, on 18 October 1970, David McDowell told me that a large portion of the text had been arranged in a binder by Agee.

[3] The composite working draft as well as additional notes and fragment which accompany the manuscript are at TxU, where they are cataloged as "Auto-

graph manuscripts." They, and other manuscripts, are published here with the consent of the library and the permission of The James Agee Trust.

⁴ The phrase "Lead as now" occurs many times in the notes—always at the head of lists of episodes.

⁵ "Autograph manuscripts."

⁶ *Partisan Review,* V (August-September 1938), pp. 22-25.

⁷ (Boston: Houghton Mifflin Company, 1968), p. 125.

⁸ James Harold Flye, "Preface to The Second Edition," *The Letters of James Agee to Father Flye* (Boston: Houghton Mifflin Company, 1971), p. viii.

⁹ See my "The Manuscript and Text of James Agee's *A Death in the Family,*" *Papers of the Bibliographical Society of America,* LXV (Third Quarter 1971), pp. 257-266.

¹⁰ "A Note on This Book," p. [ii].

¹¹ I call it "Dream Sequence" in "Agee in the Forties: Unpublished Poetry and Fiction," *Texas Quarterly,* XI (Spring 1968), pp. 38-46.

¹² It is important to note that "Dream Sequence" does not physically resemble first-draft material; in many ways it seems nearly finished. There are phrases changed and added, but there also are entire sheets with practically no changes.

¹³ Pages 121-123.

¹⁴ *Letters of James Agee to Father Flye,* p. 77.

¹⁵ "Dream Sequence," p. 45.

¹⁶ *Ibid.,* p. 41.

¹⁷ "Notes and Fragments."

¹⁸ "Dream Sequence," p. 45.

¹⁹ Compare pp. 19-22 of the novel with pp. 38-43 of "Dream Sequence."

²⁰ "Notes and Fragments."

²¹ *A Death in the Family,* p. 335.

²² "Notes and Fragments."

²³ *A Death in the Family,* p. 80, and "Working Draft.

²⁴ "Notes and Fragments."

²⁵ Pages 124-125.

²⁶ "Working draft."

²⁷ In "Agee in the Forties," pp. 47-55.

²⁸ "Working draft."

²⁹ Another of Agee's notes with the "Working draft" raises the question, "Go back into short novella length on the father and mother? and troubles of marriage?

The Manuscript and the Text for
James Agee's *A Death in the Family*

Collation of the composite manuscript of Agee's unfinished, posthumously published novel *A Death in the Family* (1957) reveals that substantial errors exist in its text. Further, such study indicates the complexity of the editorial procedure which was demanded by the autograph manuscript. The fundamental reason for the present essay is to provide a listing of definite errors which have been incorporated into the text. But the analysis also demonstrates the varieties of editorial decision necessitated by the problematic pencil holograph.[1]

In addition to problems of regularizing spelling and punctuation Agee's editors were confronted with many variants from which they chose the final text.[2] Sometimes passages of several words were omitted. In other instances whole sections of manuscript were omitted from the novel. In each place where a substantial portion of manuscript was omitted, it was either a fragmentary portion, or it was a passage which would have conflicted with the balance of the book. Such conflict may have been either a consideration of tone, in relation to the rest of the manucript, or the existence of a more complete version which had already been chosen for incorporation. The unused chapter "Surprise," appearing as part of a group of Agee manuscripts published in the *Texas Quarterly*, illustrates how a near-finished piece of writing was rejected because it conflicted with another part of the text.[3] Pages 102-111 of the novel incorporate many of the same ideas Agee developed in that rejected passage.

An example of a part of the composite manuscript which was apparently omitted because of its difference in tone from the rest of the book is the "Dream Sequence," also edited elsewhere,[4] and which might have been intended as introduction to the novel. This passage is a surrealistic nightmare in which the narrator (Agee?) recalls the death of his father. There are many parallels in idea and phrasing between this section and the opening chapter of the novel. ("Knoxville:

Summer of 1915," the sketch which is printed as prelude to the novel, is often mistakenly assumed to be part of the manuscript.[5])

Yet another example of a section omitted by editors from the book is a short, unused, chapter which treats a discussion by Jay and Mary, Rufus's parents, about the merits of purchasing an automobile.[6] Jay's death is the result of an automobile accident. Perhaps this manuscript was omitted because it is not from the point of view of Rufus, as are the other interchapter sections which are printed in italics and stand separate from the twenty sequential chapters of the book. A portion of the book for which there exists an alternate or variant manuscript version is the chapter where Rufus is alone in darkness, and his father comforts him and sings to him. The version printed in the book is a more tightly constructed, less poetic one.

In addition to these several variant passages from which the text was established, there are also individual word variants within the manuscript. From among these variants the editors had to choose what they felt was preferable. Almost always their choice was to incorporate Agee's second, or final, word choice: the word or phrase added above his initial one. Thus in the opening chapter the phrase "horrid little Charlie Chaplin!" was first written in the draft. Later the variant "man" was written above "Charlie Chaplin." The passage is printed in the text with the variant "man!" (11:3). In the first chapter alone there are seven similar instances where such variant phrasing has been chosen. The same procedure is true for most variant passages throughout the composite text of the novel. However there are also places where the text is the result of the editor's omission of the variant wording and another editor might have chosen differently. Such matters will remain arguable, and the best phrasing within the context of the book as a whole is a matter of individual decision. But there are many places throughout the text where the variant word has been ignored. And in some of these places it can be maintained that Agee's alternate phrasing was best. In the first chapter there are four instances where the text may have been weakened by the omission of variant phrasing.

In each of those places it appears that Agee intended to provide a clearer focus from the point of view of the six-year-old protagonist, Rufus. Yet his clarification has been ignored. Thus at 15:3-4 the variant modifier "shining" is not used and the original less vivid word "bright" is used. At 16:25 the sentence "You don't brag about smartness if your son is brave" was emended in the manuscript with the variants "talk" for "brag" and "boy" for "son." Agee's variant should have been chosen. It is essential for the coherence of the passage as a whole, especially because it is shortly before made clear that Rufus does not understand what "to brag" means. Similarly at page 17:17-18, the original phrase "an exhausted butterfly" is retained, but above that phrase Agee had written the perhaps more explicit description "moth's wing." Still another example occurs at 18:26 where the variant "idling" is ignored in favor of the earlier-written word "quiet." These examples are meant to illustrate the way the text for the entire novel has been established. Here illustrations are limited to the first chapter because it is clear that an editor's choice had to be a subjective one. A complete list would only emphasize the unfinished state of the manuscript. The fact remains that other editors might have chosen a different combination of variants rather than what is combined to make what is printed as Agee's novel.

To suggest further the state of the text, it should be pointed out that there are also passages which result from a combination of both original and variant. For example, in the manuscript for the opening chapter, the phrase "part bare clay" occurs with the word "rubbed" written above it and the word "slick" written below. In this instance the editorial decision was to incorporate only one of the variants in the printed text. The phrase which results is "part rubbed bare clay" (17:33). Another example of this irregularity of editorial procedure is the following where editors were confronted with a variant but included it as well as the original phrase. The sentence "He had no business phoning" is accompanied in manuscript by the variant words above "was a perfect fool to phone." Here both passages are fully incorporated into the text with the addition of the word "He" to the variant which then provides two separate sentences (128:25-26).

Of course there are numerous places in the text where punctuation and spelling are regularized, and other minor editorial changes such as pronoun reference or paragraphing are also incorporated throughout the finished text. The names of characters as they appear in the printed work were changed by editors to avoid the use of real names, such as members of Agee's family. Such changes are to be expected since the book was obviously not finished. But, in addition, several omissions of phrases or sentences occur. Here, also, it is perhaps a matter of editorial decision about what is most appropriate, and it is arguable whether these omissions differ in essence from the editorial changes of regularization which have been imposed upon the manuscript. But each of the selected omissions listed below may have, it seems to me, harmed the book. It must also be acknowledged that there are equally as many "omissions" which stand as evidence of prudential editing. Each of the omissions listed below is representative of the kinds of changes that the text has undergone, and other examples might be provided. Had such words and phrases been retained the integrity, and perhaps effectiveness, of the text would have been improved.

Page:line	book	manuscript
13:7	streetcar ,"mad	streetcar, and "mad
25:30-31	exaggerate	exaggerate, do
43:12	places	places. (he ran his tongue over his teeth).
50:27	her uncomfortable	her intensely uncomfortable
52:4	his	and his
57:19	*Oh, God! God! God! God!*	*"Oh God! God! God! God! God!*
120:30-31	bitter incredulity	bitter sardonic incredulity
149:7	sipped	sipped continuously
161:26-27	breath	breath. There wasn't.
177:10	to.	to of.
250:23	twiggy	gray twiggy
250:26	*away!"*	*away*! He shook her.
252:15	wind	strong [variant] violent wind
269:25	him	him with suspicion
271:23	group.	group. So that was what instantly meant. Right off like that. He had thought it meant not feeling anything.
273:11	body.	body, my Uncle Andrew says.
275:5	stand.	stand, and the ashtray with weighted straps, and two pipes.
280:21-22	them,	them, like his mother said,
288:33	orphan, or	orphan maybe you had to be French or Belgian to be one, for he never heard people talk about German orphans but there must be some. Then there were orphans: in asylums, but they must be like crazy people. Or did your father and mother have to be killed in the war. If you were to be an orphan would people *envy* you for being, or

Page:line	book	manuscript
319:18	had seen	had ever seen
327:31	had and,	had, his head in a regular spasm, and

Agee's handwriting is very small and difficult to decipher and all of the manuscript is written with an often blunt lead pencil, usually on porous paper. Most of the paper is either newsprint or "second copy" yellow paper. These facts of illegibility may have partially contributed to the peculiarities of the text as it has been established. Many clear errors exist in the text which are the results of a misreading of Agee's script, or of errors in proofreading. Sometimes these errors make only minor differences in meaning. Often, however, a correct reading clarifies the passage.

To demonstrate the kinds of definite errors which have, perhaps inadvertently, been incorporated into the text, only the first chapter is here discussed. There are ten places in the opening chapter where there has been a certain misreading of the manuscript. One could assume that these changes are editorial ones; but in each of these instances, there is no doubt that Agee wrote another word (or phrase) than the one printed, and that the text is in error. At 14:16-17 the word "feature" is used instead of the manuscript's "picture." This does not cause any serious change in the sense of the passage. Similarly, several of the other misreadings in the first chapter do not change the sense of the passages in which they occur. But in other instances the errors most certainly do damage meaning.

A loss in precision results with the omission of "in" which should follow "turned" in the phrase at 15:30. The action of movement through doors is less clearly presented with the omission. At 16:3 "come" is obviously a typographical error which should be "came." At 17:23 Agee's choice of the word "flinched" inadvertently has become "flicked." This weakens the phrase, a description of a signal light's changing color as apprehended by Rufus. At 18:12 the manuscript's "fall" has become "face." This does not make sense because Rufus and his father are looking out over a hill, and are unable to see its "face" at that moment. The error at 18:14 is even more serious. Here the sound of the freight cars being moved in a rail yard is described. The manuscript's "rattled" is printed as "settled." At 18:22 the word "journey" is used instead of the word Agee chose: "privacy." At 18:29 the manuscript's "for" has inadvertently become "or." This omission makes the ritual action of smoking a cigarette less obvious. The manuscript suggests that a regular pattern was followed on evenings such as those described. "Usually . . . for a few minutes before going home, Rufus' father smoked." Later in the same description of the father's gesture of placing his hat over his knee, the manuscript's "point" is not used, and instead "front" is substituted at 21:4. Lastly, the word "cranking" is misprinted at 22:8 as "creaking," and this too changes the sense of the passage.

The following listing of differences between the holograph manuscript and the text of the novel indicates clear mistakes. Although the book has gone through several printings it does not appear that any alterations have been made from the first printing. Not even obvious typographical errors have been changed.

Page:line	book	manuscript
14:16-17	feature	picture
15:30	turned	turned in
16:3	come	came
17:23	flicked	flinched
18:12	face	fall
18:14	settled	rattled
18:22	journey	privacy
18:29	or	for
21:4	front	point
22:8	creaking	cranking
24:1 + 3:	residence	res dence
24:27	fer this,	from thur [for "from there"]
27:4	break	broke
27:5	oldest	eldest
27:20	hypercritical	hypocritical
33:22	won't . . .	isn't
43:7	blocked	blacked
44:13	adherence	coherence
49:9	down	alone
57:10	well	we
68:13	comforting	comfort in
83:32	not ever	never
84:26-27	rare monsters beyond rare monsters,	ravenousness beyond ravenousness,
94:12	even	ever
95:10	even	ever
98:2	gently	gentle
110:29	the	dis
127:32	"No." I said, "*Have*	"No, I said: Have

Page:line	book	manuscript
129:30	Jay	Joel
132:31	cross	iron
136:4	the	she
141:22	Oh	"Oh. I dont' think . . ."
	"I don't think . . ."	
164:27	paralyzed . . .	—pparalyzed . .
166:10	continued	contained
197:34	contact	instant
198:8	among	during
201:15	crushed	cracked
208:26	fists	fist
213:8	know	knew
214:18	that	this
220:18	asked	acted
228:1	pocked	pecked
231:4	giving	given up
233:33	chains	chain
234:31	file	pile
237:22	to	towards
242:29	butcher	butch
252:11	sneezed	squeezed
255:7	wet	limp
261:16	bagan	began
262:5	little	long
277:3	alone	lone
277:32	me	*me*
280:24	knows	knew
307:34	self-completedness	self-completeness
314:1	amongst	upon
316:12	stuck	struck
317:1	came back	drew near
318:18	footstep	footsteps
319:30	stranger	strange
320:10	with	in
323:10	even	over

It is clear then that the printed text contains errors as well as editorial alteration of what Agee wrote. While the nature of the unfinished manuscript made it necessary that the editors make omissions from the manuscript, mistakes which should have been avoided are incorporated.

In a recent *PBSA* note (64, 84-98) which compares the serialization of Agee's novel with the book printing, Kenneth Curry has made some good suggestions about problems with the text. I have verified several of the readings which he suggested call for correction. Instances of errors he cites are included in the preceding listing. But the following readings, which he suggests are also perhaps in error, are printed exactly as in manuscript:

120:18	"got from"
132:4	"whatever is"
134:27	"fire"
137:11	"were," The comma *is* necessary for the sense of the passage.
221:15	The period is correct. Agee intended two sentences.

In the following readings Curry suggests that other punctuation would be advantageous; yet because of the "colloquial nature of the conversation" a purely "grammatical approach is not possible." There are problems with these passages, but if the manuscript had been followed in the first and third readings the text would have remained clear. In the second example Agee's punctuation has been correctly retained, and the passage is clear as it is printed.

117:6	The second comma is omitted in manuscript, not the first.
122:25	A comma appears in manuscript; no new sentence is needed.
125:2	No need for a period. Manuscript includes one comma after "twenty-four."

In two additional readings, as Curry suggests, added punctuation would clarify the passages:

125:10	A comma after "far"; none appears in manuscript.
218:11	The question mark absent from the text, is omitted in the manuscript.

Each of the readings cited above stands as an illustration of the unfinished state of the book and of the difficulties faced by the editors of *A Death in the Family*. Further editing, it is certain, still needs to be done.

What is clear from a study of the working manuscript and the text is that the editors were forced to choose from variants. They also imposed regularization upon the spelling, paragraphing, and punctuation of the unfinished manuscript. Because of editorial decision some entire sections of manuscript have been omitted from the text. Whether all of these omissions are necessary remains debatable. In addition, omission of variant words and phrases has occurred in the text. Many of these omissions might have been retained. Variants were treated individually, and while Agee's second or final choice was usually incorporated, this was not always the procedure adopted. The result is that many passages are weakened. Finally, and most importantly, several clear misreadings of Agee's difficult script (or poor proofreading) have resulted in the incorporation of errors which demand correction.

Notes

[1] The composite autograph manuscript working draft for *A Death in the Family* (New York: McDowell Obolensky, Inc., 1957) is in the library of the University of Texas. It consists of 201 autograph pages; and there are an additional 120 pages of variant manuscript. Of this variant manuscript 98 pages are duplicate, alternate or fragmentary pages for the novel; the remaining 22 pages constitute a series of notes and summary of Agee's plans for the work. This material is used with the permission of the James Agee Trust.

[2] Catalogued: *A Death in the Family*: composite autograph manuscript working draft with autograph emendations 201 pp. c. 1948-   , University of Texas Library.

[3] "Surprise" is part of "Agee in the forties: Unpublished Poetry and Fiction," *Texas Quarterly*, 11, No. 1 (1968), pp. 47-55; edited by Victor A. Kramer.

[4] "Agee in the Forties: Unpublished Poetry and Fiction," *op. cit.*, pp. 38-46.

[5] "Knoxville: Summer of 1915" originally appeared in *Partisan Review*, 5 (August-September 1938), pp. 22-25.

[6] *A Death in the Family*, autograph working draft, incomplete with autograph emendations, 94 pp. c. 1948, University of Texas Library.

VI

Synthesis Through Detail

Urban and Rural Tension in
A Death in the Family

I

A Death in the Family is autobiographical because it is about the death of James Agee's father, but it is also a book which expands into the public domain because of its exploration of the country-city conflict central to American experience from post Civil War days into the present. That this conflict is of central significance for Agee's book is the result of his personal experiences, for he was born in Knoxville, Tennessee, in 1909 when that city, though a town of only 30,000, was rapidly becoming an urban center. Still, Knoxville possessed enough of a rural flavor to remain clearly countrified in Agee's mind during his subsequent years in New York City.[1] His fictionalization of the crucial period in his life when his father died documents a period when many American lives were still determined by both the rural and town backgrounds of their families. *A Death in the Family* is, therefore, more than just a private remembrance because it clearly documents a period when much of American culture was in balance with both country and city characteristics.

When Agee wrote this autobiographical novel he attempted to catch the flavor of the time when his family was in a state of tension with ties to both the rural past and the urban future. Interestingly, the novel reflects distrust of and affection for both country and city. Agee evokes a moment in America's history when it was poised between a knowledge of a simpler past (or one which appeared to be) and the more demanding future. The novel is unusual because Agee attempts to document that past, but without the philosophical implications of writers ranging from Norris and Dreiser to Hemingway and Faulkner who have a naturalistic vein in their fiction. Agee simply attempts to suggest the beauty of a time past without being sentimental, yet the result of his procedure is a lament for a loss of balanced qualities which once made up an earlier culture, a loss brought about by the absorption of country people into cities.

Agee had begun to write about his memories of Knoxville while he was a sixteen-year-old student at Phillips Exeter Academy. Already at that early time his father's death haunted him.[2] Significantly, his "Knoxville: Summer of 1915," often assumed to be part of *A Death in the Family,* was already written in 1936, when Agee was only twenty-seven. "Knoxville" is a poetic sketch, largely about Agee's family, and especially his father. Also of significance is that by 1937 Agee had written "The House," in which he chose as setting a city about the size of "Knoxville or Chattanooga," and as might be expected, his imagined house resembles his grandparents' home in Knoxville, and a father is notably absent. Similarly, when Agee recalled earlier experiences related to remembrances in *Let Us Now Praise Famous Men,* his mind flashed back to years when he had been a fatherless adolescent in Knoxville. All of Agee's important fiction is autobiographical, and it progresses backward to his earliest remembered years. The book preceding *A Death in the Family, The Morning Watch,* is an evocation of a high point of religious emotion for a boy of twelve, and its setting is St. Andrew's, the mountain school, near Sewanee, Tennessee, where Agee was a student for five years.[3] Preceding that work is the little-known "1928 Story" set in that year, an autobiographical remembrance from the point of view of the mature artist (Agee in the late nineteen-forties) who recalls earlier hopes and aspirations.[4]

As Agee, the writer, grew older he became more aware of how he had been formed under the influence of his mother, and in the absence of a father with close country ties. His father, Hugh James Agee, had come of a mountain family, and he embodied many of the rural qualities of persons who had left farms and become urbanized. Agee's mother came of a different and more urban background. She was the daughter of a prominent businessman, and a university graduate. She was interested in art, music, and, even more significantly, the Church. One important difference between Agee's parents was an interest in formal religion fundamental for the mother, yet not apparently of much importance for Agee's father.

In *A Death in the Family* the religion (or religiosity) of the fictional mother is a basic ingredient in her reaction to the death of

her husband. Her reliance upon the Church, symbolized harshly by
Father Jackson, stands both structurally and thematically in conflict
with the early parts of the book when the true father is present.
Especially for the children of the book, something seems unnatural
and frightening in a man like Father Jackson, a letter-of-the-law-
religious, who refuses to provide a complete burial service for Jay, the
father, because he is not a believer. Rufus and his sister sense they
cannot trust Father Jackson the minute he appears at the door to
comfort their mother. In contrast to this cold priest Agee draws
portraits of several strong country men.

Rufus's father is appealing precisely because he is independently strong; but it is apparent that Rufus will become more reliant
upon guidance from his mother and organized religion after the
father's death. And the individualism, naturalness and openness,
essentially rural qualities of the father will be missed, only something
later to imagine.

The fictional parents of *A Death in the Family* had experienced
a tension in their marriage, "a gulf" which had only recently begun to
close. But the marriage was growing into a strong bond which apparently was beneficial to all the family members. The father's death
abruptly breaks that balance, and the urban, genteel qualities of the
mother promise to become dominant; Jay's active contribution to the
rearing of his children is lost with his death. The same might well be
said of cultural ties with a rural America which urban people have lost
during this century.

Just as in his novel Agee's life was inevitably formed because of
decisions of his mother. Her awareness that he needed the influence
of men teachers was partially responsible for his enrollment at St.
Andrew's; and her interest in religion simultaneously had definite
effects on Agee's own religious formation.[5] After five years at St.
Andrew's and a year of high school in Knoxville, he attended Phillips
Exeter, and Harvard. Graduating at the peak of the Depression, he
landed a job on the staff of *Fortune* magazine, and his subsequent
frustration in writing unsigned pieces for *Fortune*, and *Time*, and film
criticism for *The Nation*, and later scenarios before his early death, is
(and, has been lamented as) emblematic of problems many American
writers face. Agee's work as a professional journalist in New York
City, a place as different as imaginable from the Tennessee mountains
where his father had been reared, did not allow him sufficient time to

do "his own writing"; but all of the substantial prose works which he did complete are noteworthy because they demonstrate that he never lost his affection for the Tennessee and Knoxville of his earliest years, and Agee's major work reflects his awareness of how his important formative influences were a blending of urban and rural forces. His best writing was always the result of personal experience, his childhood, and his ties with Knoxville, and the mountains of Tennessee. For instance his recognition that, given a different set of circumstances, he might have been born into a life similar to that of tenant farmers he wrote about in *Let Us Now Praise Famous Men* is a basic part of that work's design. Similarly, *The Morning Watch* could never have been written without Agee's memories of the country school where he spent five years; and finally, *A Death in the Family*, planned as a memorial to his dead father, also grows out of Agee's realization that his memories were related to the memories of all raised under similar circumstances. Thus, *A Death in the Family* is a novel which expands outward to become representative of many lives. But to understand how the book is autobiographical one need only know that among manuscript notes are detailed lists of particular moments and events recalled from the days surrounding the father's funeral, much of which was also fictionalized.[6] The closing sequence of the book where Rufus' uncle tells him about the butterfly which settled on the coffin as it was lowered into the ground was "vaguely" remembered by Agee.[7] The same certainly is the case with other episodes such as the teasing of Rufus by older boys, and the details of the funeral.

II

As Agee was first planning *A Death*, it appears that he wanted to rely upon a technique similar to that employed in *Famous Men*. That is, he would write only about what he could remember. This is especially true of the opening and closing sections of the book and the inter-chapter material, which falls outside the main chronological sequence. But the novel developed out of a larger conflict; in a fundamental way it was Agee's mode of simultaneously remembering the past, and getting away from the horrors of the present. Agee wrote much of this book in the late forties, a time when he was especially disturbed by the use of the atomic bomb and the problem of how individuals can survive in a mass society. Both "Dedication Day" and "Scientists and Tramps" are of this period. In "1928 Story," which was written at the same time *A Death* was begun, Agee begins by outlining the disappointment and frustration which the speaker feels in not having written as much, or as well, as he might have. Such statements flow into a remembrance of earlier times, and the speaker is able to catch the beauty (and awkwardness) of earlier moments. In *A Death in the Family* Agee also took very simple events from his childhood and allowed his imagination to play over them. Some parts of his remembrance are therefore chronologically months or years in advance of the father's death. With such reference points it was possible for Agee to reconstruct the domestic love which enveloped the young Rufus, a love which combined country and city attitudes.

Agee was only six years old when his father died, thus while his book is definitely written to honor his father, it is as well an attempt to catch a moment three decades in the past. As Agee matured he came to realize that particular events and places in his childhood neighborhood had been experienced by both him and his father. For instance, the railroad viaduct, which today still bridges the valley between the business center of Knoxville and residential areas, was a specific place which Agee associated with his father. The bridge is carefully described in the fictional account of Rufus and Jay; and the evocation of that bridge is representative of the method of the entire book. The remembered past is suggested through careful attention to the "dignity of actuality." Rufus, of the book, recalls how "Whenever they walked downtown and walked back home in the evenings, they always began to walk more slowly, from about the middle of the viaduct, and as they came near [their] corner they walked more slowly still, but with purpose. . . ."[8] Through specific attention to details of place such a passage suggests how Rufus sensed the homesickness of his father.

Readers of this novel usually recall the sketch "Knoxville: Summer of 1915" which was chosen by editors as an appropriate opening for the book. Its dominant tone is one of nostalgia for an earlier quiet time; and it is one of several autobiographical or reminiscent pieces about Tennessee which were written in the thirties. Another is an experimental poem, entitled "In Memory of My Father,"[9] in which some of the same imagery employed in the novel is used; its poetic remembrance of a small child, going to sleep and comforted by the parent, is an image which suggests all children in similar circumstances. Agee's sketch, "Knoxville: Summer of 1915," similarly does an economical job of evoking an atmosphere like that Rufus and his father enjoy, such as at the beginning of the novel when they go to the movies, and walk home together, but it is not the complete mood which generated the novel. In "Knoxville" a time of harmony with nature is recalled; the cities' noises are blended with natural ones. Another mood generated the novel and is evident in an excluded passage called "Dream Sequence." There, a tension between country and city is clearly evident. Edited since the novel's publication, Agee's "Dream" begins as nightmare and suggests that only through a work of art can lasting harmony be achieved; but it is necessary for the artist first to exorcise the nightmare of urban life if the peacefulness of a remembrance like *A Death in the Family* is to be created.

"Dream Sequence" is a sketch which records the nightmare of a narrator (very much like Agee) who recalls how he found himself on a crowded city street—perhaps New York; perhaps Chattanooga—but then obviously Knoxville: "The town had certainly changed. It wasn't as he remembered it from childhood, nor did he like its looks as well as his memories of it. . . . Even the heat and sunlight of the weather was different, it was the weather of a bigger, worse, more proud and foolish city. . . ."[10] The narrator relates how he saw a group of people doing something horrible to someone, and upon approaching the crowd he knew it was John the Baptist being stoned. He decided a proper burial was in order, and he began that chore. He began pulling the corpse down the sweltering and then freezing streets—symbolism which suggests the passing of years. And as time passed, the terrain became more and more familiar. In both this "Dream" and in the opening section of the novel Agee recalls the outcroppings of limestone common to the landscape of Knoxville. A visitor to Agee's old neighborhood in Knoxville would notice the same outcroppings today.

Two things become clearer to Agee's dreamer. First, he was getting closer to the old neighborhood where he and his father used to enjoy their privacy late at night: "The corner was where he used to sit with his father and it was there of all times and places that he had known his father loved him. . . . And his father had come out of the wilderness, and it was there that the Son had best known his homesickness for the wilderness." And secondly, if the man was John the Baptist, he was somehow also the narrator's Father, and he, the Christ, had failed his father. The question is how could that failure be rectified (at least partially)? The answer is to go back into those years, by way of a work of art, and to do honor to the memory of the father by evoking as much of those times as possible.

The last pages of "Dream" possess the same calmness as the opening of the book. Agee's return to the calmness of his childhood, interrupted by the father's death, is made by way of the horrors of contemporary life, an urban life symbolized by a maddened crowd. Agee's homage to his father, then, seems to be both a recapitulation of what he remembered, and a symbolic statement about all who are drawn to the city.

There is a large amount of nostalgia in what Agee decided to do; yet it is only through such nostalgia that it is possible to achieve a perspective adequate for a vision of how rural and urban forces were once in conjunction to form moments of domestic love. Agee wanted to do honor to an earlier time. To do so his memory became as important as his imagination. It is significant to observe that in the manuscript for Agee's novel the names of real persons are used. The same is true of much of the manuscript for *The Morning Watch* and *Let Us Now Praise Famous Men*.

Agee wrote in one of his working notes that Jay, the father, was a "victim of progress." One of the variant sections for this book is a discussion between the parents about the dangers of purchasing an automobile.[11] What better symbol is there for the fragmentation of family? The marriage and its love provided an atmosphere for Rufus; and the inference is clearly to be drawn that the child drew upon the love of both parents. Thus Agee placed a high value upon the time when rural forces, and the presence of the father, were blended with city life. But Agee, and modern American culture and modern Americans, lost the strength to be gained from such a blending.

There is the possibility that had Agee lived to complete his novel, he would have written more sections which stress autobiographical remembrances of country and city. One such excluded section is a short sequence of two pages in which Rufus recalls how his father used to spit in the fireplace—much to the horror of the mother. After she had instructed Jay not to do such a thing in front of Rufus, Rufus observed Jay continued to do it only when the boy was present.[12] When Rufus is in the presence of his parents, or when he thinks about them, Agee stresses the contrast between them and the fact that both contribute important qualities which make his world secure. One section of the novel is a stream-of-consciousness monologue in which the child muses about the differences he senses between his parents: "She wore dresses, his father wore pants. Pants were what he wore too, but they were short and soft" (100). Other similar passages are incorporated throughout the text.

It is the combination of mother and father, and their differing attitudes, which allow Rufus to feel at ease. When a motoring trip to visit the father's relatives was taken, Rufus remembers it in this way: "*After dinner the babies and all the children except Rufus were laid out on the beds to take their naps, and his mother thought that he ought to lie down too, but his father said no, why did he need to, so he was allowed to stay up*" (227). And similarly, when Rufus is first introduced to his great-great-grandmother, and he kisses her, it is the mother who voices concern, and his father who says "Let her be" (240). Jay will have Rufus experience as much of the world as possible, and he tries not to be overly protective. In another episode Aunt Hannah senses that the cap Rufus wants is correct for a boy who wants to be grown up. Rufus had asked his mother for a cap, but suffered a rebuff a year earlier when she refused. We can understand with Rufus that if Jay went shopping "his father wouldn't mind" (14) if he had such a cap "even though his mother would not want him to have a cap, yet." And Hannah reflects that "Mary would have conniption fits" over Rufus' choice, but "Jay wouldn't mind" (78).

In a related way, during the opening pages of the novel when Jay and Rufus are getting ready to go see a Chaplin movie, Jay enjoys asking "What's wrong with [Charlie]?" "not because he didn't know what Mary would say, but so she would say it" (11). And then when Rufus and his father go, ritualistically, to the movies they feel all the more enclosed in each others' presence. The father is somewhat rough, a bit coarse, and country. But the mother seems overly genteel; and going to the movies is an escape from her. On the walk home Jay stops off at a saloon looking for friends from his home mountain area.

Rufus senses that he needs both parents but he is without such abstract knowledge. Agee looking back over his life, and his remembrance of those years, also saw the need for the balance provided by both parents. The picture which we are given of Rufus's parents is one which combines the best qualities. Where this is most apparent is the contrast in the scenes where Jay and Mary, separately, sing to Rufus. Jay loved to sing the old country songs he remembered from childhood. Rufus realized that sometimes his father joked by talking like a darky, and "*the way he sang was like a darky too, only when he sang he wasn't joking*" (99-101). And Rufus also remembered how his parents sang together, and how beautifully her clear voice combined with Jay's, but when she tried to sound like a country singer she could not do it. Rufus "liked both ways very much and best of all when they sang together and he was there with them...," but he is suddenly separated from such experience when his father is killed.

Throughout the novel it is implied that Jay has accommodated himself to living in the city. The passage which describes his journey to his father's sick bed, a trip which ironically leads to his own death, points up how he must have often felt about aspects of the city. "The city thinned out," Agee wrote, and for a few minutes Jay drove through

> the darkened evidences of that kind of flea-bitten semi-
> rurality which always peculiarly depressed him: mean
> little homes, and others inexplicably new and substantial,
> set too close together for any satisfying rural privacy or
> use, too far, too shapelessly apart to have coherence as any
> kind of community; mean little pieces of ill-cultivated land
> behind them, and alongside the road, between them, trash
> and slash and broken sheds and rained-out billboards....
> (44)

This is the same kind of feeling almost everyone experiences (unconsciously perhaps) as movement from urban to rural is experienced. That feeling would be all the more acute if a rural background were one's origin. Then, it would seem, material progress and faith in institutions—whether governmental or religious—might be increasingly difficult to accept. Fifty years ago, when Agee's father was in his middle thirties, it would have been even more poignant a feeling.

It is made clear that the fictional family was in the habit of going into the country for a Sunday drive. The ferryman who takes Jay across the river recognizes him: "You generally always come o' Sundays, yer womurn, couple o' younguns," and Jay answers with a monosyllabic reply which reflects his country ties: "Yeahp" (45). Agee, significantly, qualifies that Jay reflected "Must be a nice job ... as he nearly always did, except of course in winter" (45). The mother clearly senses that Jay feels most comfortable in the country; and when she prepares Jay's breakfast in the early morning, she does it the way she imagines a mountain woman might.

A revealing interchange in the novel occurs during one of the family trips to visit relatives. On that Sunday the parents attempt to figure out how old the Great-great-grandmother might be, and Mary comments "'—*why she's almost as old as the country, Jay.*'" Jay's reply suggests much about how these parents think. He immediately meditates on the natural world—the geological fact of the mountains; but the mother thinks of the country's government. Dealing in abstract concepts is not Jay's ordinary mode of thought. He deals more immediately within the concrete; and it is for such reasons that he enjoys being with Rufus and singing old songs. There are many manuscript variants for the section about singing which demonstrate Agee's fascination and respect for this subject. During one of his evenings of song Jay recalls how his own mother used to sing to him (and how those times are gone);[13] yet how through one's children they can be repeated, at least a little bit:

> Just one way, you do get back home. You have a boy or a
> girl of your own and now and then you remember, and you
> know how they feel. . . ." (94)

III

There is yet another way, and that is the artist's. In one of the working notes for the novel Agee recalled that on one of the mornings surrounding his father's funeral he and his sister were taught how to read the comics—arms just so, legs up, and bellies on the floor, and he added a comment that such actions implied archetypal actions performed by those unaware of what they were doing. Agee's entire fictionalization is archetypal in this manner. Thus other parts of this book work similarly to suggest either the fragmentation of family or the loss of rural virtues. Agee's novel suggests a wider pattern of fathers absorbed by the city, then senselessly killed, with their families then destined to be formed in their absence.

The central theme of Agee's book is domestic love—a subject that seems particularly unpromising for a novelist in the middle part of the twentieth century. But delicate domestic love, which has been experienced by millions of families, is what holds the remembrance together. The family has always provided comfort and nurture, but in a society like today's, the family seems best described by Henry Adams in his delineation of the centrifugal forces of the society. Family members spin away from each other as external activities become more pronounced. However, each action and gesture of love is unique, and as these individual acts are performed they have value within a unique framework. It was such a realization along with the conviction that city forces were becoming stronger that prompted Agee to "go back into those years."

The precision which Agee achieved in the writing of this book has sometimes been compared to uses of the camera; it is not a novel in the ordinary sense. His language and point of view is often heavily reliant upon visual remembrance of remembered actions. The entire first chapter; the details provided about Jay's departure at three in the morning; the definiteness of Aunt Hannah and Rufus's shopping trip; and the details of the funeral itself are a few places where Agee's descriptive powers focus upon particularities. Because he so respected his remembered world his fiction was easily adapted into a drama and film. In the play and film as well as the novel, one is assured that one is witness to a way of life which is passing. It has sometimes been remarked that Agee's book is not a novel at all, but really a long poem similar to the multi-faceted remembrances of *Let Us Now Praise Famous Men*. This is correct and Agee's lyrical writing arrests moments which would fade away with no memorial if he chose not to write of them, but because Agee evokes particularities he documents that earlier era. It is appropriate to mention that the Agee home had been razed by the time the film, *All The Way Home*, was made in the middle 1960's, and in its place in Knoxville is to be found a set of apartments labelled "The James Agee Apartments."

As one is reminded of the change which a town like Knoxville has undergone, one is able to focus on an earlier time when many opposing forces were still clearly in productive tension. The little town imagined in this novel was small enough so that after Jay's death Mary's family could simply walk over to her house. Yet, as has been suggested, it was already a city where Jay could not feel completely at home. Throughout the novel the sounds of railroad cars interrupt domestic privacy and quiet. For example, at the end of the chapter, when Jay has departed to visit his sick father, Agee ends with the sentence "A streetcar passed; Catherine cried" (54) which implies how the city, with its trolleys and automobiles, was affecting lives.

Agee wrote that Jay was a "victim of progress." He is, and so is the family which might have developed differently had he lived and been able to exert influence in the formation of Rufus beyond his first few years. But Jay died as did that era of American history—but not without inspiring the work of art which is *A Death in the Family*. And through the novelist's art that somewhat more balanced era remains alive.

Notes

[1] See Agee's story in *Fortune* about the Tennessee Valley Authority where he describes Knoxville, 11 (May 1935), pp. 93-98 and 140-153.

[2] For instance, Agee published a poem about a widow on Christmas eve, *The Phillips Exeter Monthly*, 30 (May 1926), p. 180.

[3] See my "James Agee's Unpublished Manuscript and His Emphasis on Religious Emotion in *The Morning Watch*," *Tennessee Studies in Literature*, 17 (1972), pp. 159-164.

[4] "1928 Story" is part of "Agee in the Forties: Unpublished Poetry and Fiction," edited by Victor A. Kramer, *Texas Quarterly*, 11 (Spring 1968), pp. 23-37.

[5] Interestingly Mrs. Agee published a book of religious poems while she was in residence at St. Andrews. See the discussion of Laura Tyler Agee's *Songs of the Way* (St. Andrew's Tennessee: n.p., 1922) in Charles W. Mayo's unpublished doctoral dissertation "James Agee: His Literary Life and Work" (Peabody, 1969), p. 22+ff.

[6] Peter Ohlin's *Agee* (New York: Obolensky, 1966) discusses the novel in terms of how Agee transfigures reality. While Ohlin had no access to manuscript materials, and does not mention the urban-rural theme in the book, his discussion does provide insight into how Agee fictionalizes ordinary experience.

[7] Agee's working notes for *A Death in the Family*, now at the Humanities Research Center of the University of Texas at Austin, show that he, at least early in the book's composition, thought about incorporating many details about family outings. The James Agee Trust has granted permission for my use of these materials.

See my article "*A Death in the Family* and Agee's Projected Novel," *Proof*, 3 (1973), pp. 139-154, also reprinted in this book.

[8] *A Death in the Family* (New York: Grosset and Dunlap, 1967), p. 18. All subsequent references are within parentheses.

[9] *Collected Poems of James Agee* (Boston: Houghton Mifflin Company, 1968), p. 59.

[10] "Dream Sequence" is part of "Agee in the Forties," pp. 38-46.

[11] See my article "Premonition of Disaster: An Unpublished Section for Agee's *A Death in the Family*," *Costerus* New Series, 1 (1974), pp. 83-93.

[12] See pp. 149-150 of *Proof* article.

[13] My article, "Agee's Use of Regional Material in *A Death in the Family*," *Appalachian Journal*, I (Autumn 1972), pp. 72-80, includes a variant version of this section.

Skepticism About Art and Audience

I

While he was often called a born writer, James Agee frequently expressed skepticism about the possibilities of language, especially within a society where materialism remained the core of activities; such skepticism manifested itself even within his earliest writing, exploratory and satirical pieces written at Phillips Exeter and Harvard. Perhaps because Agee remained so aware of the need to write well, but also of the difficulties inherent in successful use of language, some of his best performances were oral, accompanied only by gesture, and for which no draft copy would ever be made. His ambivalence about language and the problems of reading certainly contributed to his interest in film; ultimately, his judgments about language, culture, and the responsibilities of all users of language are fundamental to his best writing, a body of work often critical of his contemporary civilization. Agee's awareness of the problems of language—a skepticism perhaps early reinforced by his admiration of I. A. Richards, one of his teachers at Harvard—in interaction with his life and work as a writer in New York City, combined to generate a significant body of writing.

Agee once insisted that all work is a "cheated ruin" but the thing through which anyone stays alive. To an important degree his career as a writer in New York was both his livelihood and ruin, but it was as well his stimulation and reward. We know Agee was already aware in the mid-1930s that continued work for *Fortune* or *Time* was a trap. His insistence that he had to be free of such regular obligations emphasizes his conviction that he wanted to pursue his own writing; yet when we look at his career as a whole we cannot ignore the fact that the very writing he did as a journalist served as the apprenticeship for his best prose. Agee's concern about the difficulties of using language, and his skepticism about recreating the world he observed through art, combined to lead him beyond conventional uses of language in reportage or fiction.

Agee's earliest work indicates that he could write conventional poetry and prose, but it is quite clear that throughout the 1930s he felt a need for developing other methods. Such facts account for both the fun and the failure of his long poem "John Carter," as well as the accomplishment and frustration of his writing for *Fortune*. Both that long poem and Agee's unsigned journalism reflect a fundamental division which remained within his mind—a desire to write, yet an uncertainty about how best to do so.

As he began his employment at *Fortune* in the midst of the Depression, he was surely happy to have that job; but later, he was not completely joking when he expressed a wish to confront the "Founder" of *Time* with a machine gun. Agee performed a competent job at *Fortune*, and for a while a joke even circulated at the magazine's offices in the Chrysler Building that founder-editor Luce had considered sending Agee back to Harvard to the Business School. But Agee had taken his job at *Fortune* with little intention of staying; as early as 1932 he had applied for a Guggenheim with the hope that its $2,500 might support him for a sustained period in France. One of the projects he hoped to finish was the long poem "John Carter," which was, in Agee's words, to be "a complete appraisal of contemporary civilization, and a study of the Problem of Evil." In that poem he wanted to give contemporary language variety and vitality, and to write poetry which would hold modern attention. A light tone, he hoped, would maintain interest and enforce serious passages, but also allow acceptance of the moral and religious intention. Privately, he indicated doubts to Dwight Macdonald as he began what he called a "cockery narrative poem." Agee wrote:

> On the whole, a flop, but I'm fool enough to have faith in the idea: vaguely—that I can take a somewhat stock bawdy situation, fit to characters common to Chaucer & to Mid-western "Realistic" novels—and make something of it. Chaucer at best wouldn't vomit on [it]. Only it would seem to take practice, very careful study, and about 10 times the talent & five times the guts I have to do it.*

---

* The James Agee Trust has granted permission for the use of the manuscript materials referred to in this paper; I am also thankful to Dwight Macdonald for providing me with copies of Agee's correspondence to him.

In conception "John Carter" was as ambitious as *Let Us Now Praise Famous Men*, but finally only two long sections (about forty pages) were completed. As Robert Fitzgerald has noted, the "savage examination of certain Episcopalian attitudes and decor—and even more, the sheer amount of this—indicates quite adequately how 'Church' and 'organized religion' . . . bothered his mind." Agee's satire attacks the complexity of a society which has lost reverence for tradition; much of the verse emphasizes the hypocrisy and deceit which inform high-church Episcopalianism. American attitudes toward business, advertising, and sex are also objects of attention. Usually the attack is presented through an amalgam of language, a hilarious combination of cliché, advertising jargon, and parody. A typical two lines: "True lust will triumph over indigestion;/God moves in mysterious ways, I hear." The unfinished "John Carter" stands as an indication of its writer's vast ambition, and it is also evidence that much energy and enthusiasm were devoted to projects other than staff work for *Fortune*. Yet Agee clearly remained unsure of his method.

Dwight Macdonald recalls that Agee was regarded as *Fortune*'s specialist in "rich, beautiful prose," and Agee's journalistic work reveals the personality which clearly informs his style. Articles such as "The Drought" and "The American Roadside" possess an expansiveness of vision; while they remain factual, they reveal Agee's consciousness of the possibilities everywhere available for analysis through a critical inquiry. His article about the Tennessee Valley Authority takes the reader back to the hills of Tennessee and to the small city of Knoxville, which he remembered from childhood, and describes how the surrounding area was changing with the arrival of the Tennessee Valley Authority. In still other articles, for instance "August at Saratoga," Agee concentrates on providing accurate images: streets, deserted, early in the morning "strangely empty as a new-made corpse of breath."

Agee wrote twenty-five articles for *Fortune*, but usually not on subjects he would have chosen. It was only an assignment in 1936 to go to Alabama to do a survey of cotton tenantry that gave him a chance to do the type of writing which he felt was pioneering. It was not that he did not write well as a journalist, or that he could not admire the accomplishments of conventional modes of writing. It was rather that he saw so much else that might be done. For example, in a letter he wrote to Macdonald in 1936 to say that he was enjoying Henry James's

The American, his qualifying remarks reveal a fundamental stance and suggest the kind of writing Agee did best:

> I can imagine that I w[oul]d equally enjoy & have to finish anything he ever wrote that I once started, on the other hand am not so dead sure I will start anymore. Possibly more sense in reading less-good contemporaries who by hook, crook or otherwise open up a little more of future: though meanwhile name me 5 who do.

Agee's own "Plans for Work," which accompanied his second application for a Guggenheim in October 1937, must have seemed to the selection committee much too much concerned with methods which might "open up the future." Included was an outline for forty-seven separate proposed projects; predictably, no fellowship was forthcoming. Agee explained how he planned to do various pieces of fiction, notes on photography, music, theater, and revues. Five of his proposals were suggestions for fiction; significantly, he also wished to write serious stories "whose whole intention is the direct communication of the intensity of common experience." Beyond any concern with traditional forms of writing are suggestions such as the following:

> [1] *A "new" style of use of the imagination.*
> . . . the effort is to suspect the mind of invention and to invent nothing . . .
> [2] *City streets. Hotel Rooms. Cities.*
> . . . Again, the wish is to consider such *in their own terms.* . . .
> [3] *Analyses of miscommunication; the corruption of ideas.*

Still more proposals contained outlines for various kinds of analysis, poetry, even collection of data; enough is suggested to keep scores of writers busy for years. A dominant idea in many of these proposals emphasize Agee's desire for new methods to analyze everyday realities, but in ways which would include the subjective. Agee realized that a tremendous amount was to be learned from collection and analysis of letters, photographs, and public comments. Thus he argued that court records and newspaper columns were revealing as "self-indictments," and he suggested that a record of a room "in its own terms" has a value different from any use of it as "atmosphere" in fiction. He was fascinated with the possibilities which the ordinary world offered both for analysis and a challenge to communication. Such suggestions reveal his dissatisfaction with accepted methods of writing about fact.

Much of what he actually accomplished in the 1930s is an extension of this fascination with the complexity of ordinary emotion and consciousness. He knew that there were many critical projects simply waiting to be recorded. Why not write, he had suggested, a "new type of 'horror' story" about the horror "that can come of objects and their relationships." Such "stories," not traditional fiction, would communicate the intensity of common experience and would concentrate "on what the senses receive and the memory and context does with it." Such proposals are the logical outgrowth of what he had observed as early as "They That Sow. . . ," a story written at Harvard; more importantly, these plans are steps in a progression toward *Famous Men*.

Similarly, his poetry, which appeared after 1934, also demonstrates change. "From now on kill America out of your mind," the "Lyric" published in 1937, seems a set of instructions for his better work of later years. Its speaker suggests that little is to be achieved from thinking of abstractions associated with nation. To think of individuals and "the land/Mutually shapen as a child" is better. Another poem, "Summer Evening," apparently based on specific memories, is successful because it evokes an ordinary evening in a small town. Such poetry signals an imaginative return to the quiet which Agee associated with childhood. His beautifully evocative "Sunday: Outskirts of Knoxville, Tenn." is another example of this new mode of writing with a concentration of specifics, the kind of concentration that became the focus of the masterwork *Let Us Now Praise Famous Men*. Prose pieces, like the sketch "Knoxville: Summer of 1915," which Agee thought of as an unconventional short story, and his analysis of Brooklyn, rejected for publication by *Fortune* in 1939, further prepared him for writing about his personal experiences with cotton farmers in Alabama during the summer of 1936. But such concentration on the immediacy of things observed also intensified Agee's skepticism about the writer's ability to honor actuality.

II

Agee's awareness of the difficulties writers face when confronting the facts of living is reflected in the "Intermission: Conversation in the Lobby" section of *Famous Men,* a section which consists of answers to questions which had been sent to writers by the *Partisan Review* in 1939. The editors had returned Agee's answers with the curt comment: "'No publisher is under any obligation to publish an attack upon himself.'" The answers to the *Partisan Review* questions reveal much about the method of *Famous Men* and about the impact on Agee of conventional thinking about writing. Asked if a writer should use his abilities to attack the enemy if war came, Agee was perplexed, since in his opinion he had always been "at war with the enemy." The entire text for *Famous Men* is part of the battle. It may even be true, as Walker Evans once suggested, that Agee calculatedly overdid the *Fortune* story version of the Alabama report precisely so that it could never be printed by *Fortune.*

When Agee learned that he and Evans were to prepare a story about tenant farming, he was enthusiastic about that prospect because it promised to provide substantial material which would utilize his theories about nonfiction, but he also had doubts before he ever made the journey south about being able to write adequately. He felt his Alabama assignment was the "best break" he received while at *Fortune;* yet he expressed "considerable doubts" about an ability to bring it off in relation to "theory."

Those theories merit our attention. As early as 1937, he speculated how he might handle this diverse material: "Any given body of experience is sufficiently complex and ramified to require . . . more than one mode of reproduction: it is likely that this one will require many, including some that will extend writing and observing methods . . . the job is perhaps chiefly a skeptical study of the nature of reality and of the false nature of re-creation and of communication." The word "skeptical" is at the heart of Agee's procedure. Almost predictably, when the book was published, just as America was entering the Second World War, no one seemed particularly interested in such an experiment in communication. Today (while still little read) the book is acknowledged a classic, a canonization which Agee would find alarming.

Agee's text is both a literary work and not a literary work. The

The method of reporting the "*un*imagined," in gestation for years, finally included the total experience—including biography, how the book was set into type, personal guilt, dull facts, and qualified imagination. (The book might have been published two years earlier had Agee not quarreled with Harper's about their requested deletion of objectionable language.)

The writer's confrontation with myriads of distortions is at the heart of the text. And a fundamental assumption which undergirds the text—ironically a work of "Art," despite Agee's insistence that it is not—is that any attempt to provide an accurate record of what was observed was doomed. The basic notion which had to be communicated was that distinct persons and events were apprehended. But Agee knew that he had been definitely affected by what he experienced, and *his* reactions were equally important. *Famous Men*'s aesthetic, therefore, focuses attention on detail as remembered, but modified by the writer's reflection. Agee knew that what he experienced could never be fully communicated; he even says that, if it were possible, there would be "no writing at all." But Agee also remembered what Beethoven had said, "'He who understands my music can never know unhappiness again,'" and he indicates that he must state the same of his own perception, while "performance . . . is another matter." The text finally concerns itself not only with sharecroppers, or even with workers in the United States, but with all who work in the world.

Agee's insistence on being present throughout his book violates all the then accepted criteria for journalism and documentaries, as well as for Art with a capital *A*. A section-by-section analysis of his text reveals how he systematically voices questions of skepticism about communication. There is hardly a page in the book where he does not imply the difficulty of what is attempted. The basic method remains one of presenting facts, but Agee sought extreme documentation because he was convinced that man's corruption of sight is so severe that an exaggeration of technique was needed. The three opening scenes are an indication of Agee's own guilt concerning his involvement in the entire experiment, but they are also severely detailed reports about what was experienced. The almost baroque "A Country Letter" goes out of its way to emphasize how the reporter was part of the experience; and the entire section "Some Findings," while full of facts, never lets readers forget the difficulty of writing about such facts. In the parts of the book which provide Agee's findings and comments, he writes about money, shelter, clothing, education, and work. His method is one that constantly emphasizes the division within his mind: Agee clearly respects language and uses it carefully, but simultaneously he doubts the possibility of ever communicating the essence of what had been undergone.

Famous Men is therefore a sustained example of Agee's combination of information about self and particular events observed. The text is also often a parody of journalistic methods. Agee so concentrates on details that the reader is almost sickened, overwhelmed with "actuality." Through the text's emphasis, and as well its relationship to music, Agee refuses to let readers forget the complexity of what was being attempted. This is not to suggest that he was overly apologetic about what he was writing; but he realized that much could be implied about the Alabama experience if he constantly emphasized the difficulty of reporting that truth, and, by implication, any truth. Agee hoped that Famous Men was only a beginning. He originally projected three volumes, and, further, notebook material makes it clear that he thought about using the techniques developed for Famous Men for analogous projects. In a sense his film criticism became that analysis.

Throughout the 1940s Agee's writing was often about, or for, the movies. His film criticism can best be described as an extension of the method of skepticism developed for Famous Men—most importantly as a procedure for the revelation of culture as observed through traits of one particular facet of the society, film. Also, during the 1940s Agee became increasingly aware of the complexity of the individual's struggle within modern society. That awareness manifested itself in two ways: an overt skeptical commentary ("Dediction Day," "Scientists and Tramps," and "A Mother's Tale") and, more importantly, as a movement by Agee toward autobiographical remembrances. His "1928 Story," probably written about 1947, is an example of Agee's critical attitude toward society working in harmony with his then developing autobiographical impulse. Agee's convictions about individualism had been intensified by the horrors of the atomic bomb; in his opinion the war, and the cynicism connected with it, had been too easily accepted by most Americans. His most succinct literary treatment of the demise of individualism is a satire, "Dedication Day, a rough sketch for a motion picture." This sketch satirizes an imagined dediction of a monument designed to commemorate the discovery of the atom's destructive power. "Dedication Day" is a parody of a news story such as those Agee was then doing for *Time* magazine, and beneath its surface is again reflected Agee's doubts about the relationship between language and facts. (The sketch also provides an interesting contrast to Agee's own hopes of 1934 as expressed in his poem "Dedication.")

The partly autobiographical "1928 Story" both resembles the later autobiographical fiction and catches the spontaneity and enthusiasm of an earlier time in Agee's life. "1928 Story" corroborates significant facts about Agee as writer in the 1940s. His ambivalent attitudes about the role of any artist who must use language are reflected in it. As his first sustained attempt after *Famous Men* to recreate a mood from his own life, it demonstrates that Agee could catch the beauty of earlier times. As the story opens, Irvine, a writer, listens to old records which remind him of earlier years when the same music had been heard within an altogether different atmosphere. "1928 Story" is only a minor piece, yet it helps us to appreciate all of Agee's later accomplishments and to understand his continued skepticism about what any writer sets out to accomplish. This story, just like *The Morning Watch*, is therefore a step toward *A Death in the Family*; it shows that Agee learned to focus on the particularities of his own life. The interesting point is that just as *Famous Men* grew out of Agee's work for *Fortune*, the final fiction was, apparently, to some degree the result of frustrations experienced during later years as journalist, critic, and writer in New York City.

A Death in the Family can be thought of as a continuation of Agee's dual awareness: his desire to write, but his definite skepticism about how this could be accomplished. In this, his final book, Agee's emphasis is definitely on remembrance, and less on problems inherent in writing. The word "poetic" often occurs in description of Agee's novel, and many discussions of it have emphasized how the book is more poem than novel. This is because *A Death in the Family* is primarily concerned with evoking earlier moments from Agee's own life. We know he had wanted to write about his father's death as early as age sixteen, and we remember that some of the best writing accomplished during the 1930s relies on remembrance of family. Thus, the 1936 sketch "Knoxville: Summer of 1915" was chosen by Agee's editor, David McDowell, as a prelude for *A Death in the Family*. This sketch evokes the peaceful atmosphere Rufus and his family enjoyed; however, recollection of such peacefulness is not the only thing which generated that fictional remembrance. Another mood which apparently contributed to the novel is evident in an excluded fragment that I have edited, which I call "Dream Sequence." That manuscript suggests that, through a work of art, reconciliation with the past is achieved, but the artist must first exorcise the nightmare of contemporary life before a peacefulness like that of *A Death in the Family* can be created. The closing tone of "Dream Sequence" is similar in mood to the first chapter of the novel, and both evoke a peacefulness made possible when the father and son are together. Fundamental to *A Death in the Family*'s opening chapter, which recounts a typical evening when Rufus and Jay had gone to the movies and had walked home, is a basic idea of the book: the insistence that, while one cannot be comfortable with the responsibilities of living, it is necessary to accept frustration. Agee's stress on such acceptance by different characters is the most important single thematic element in his novel. The book is as well an indication of his acceptance of his frustrations as a writer.

The final book, then, clearly autobiographical, is also a statement by Agee of his realization that each person needs to be at ease in his living. If *A Death in the Family* is about Agee's father, drawn from the mountains of Tennessee because of the promise of the city, it is also about Jim Agee, the writer, drawn to New York but frustrated in his desire to be the kind of writer he felt he might be.

III

Much of Agee's writing, as has been suggested—"Dedication" of *Permit Me Voyage*, "John Carter," *Famous Men*, and *A Death in the Family*—derives from a dissatisfaction with conventional expression. Fundamental to much of this writing is Agee's skepticism of the printed word; however, the important point remains that Agee would never have developed as the writer he did had he not been made keenly aware of the assaults on language and individualism which he felt were becoming much too common in journalism, advertising, film, and fiction. Thus the rage, just below the surface of *Famous Men*, goes hand in hand with the reverence of *A Death*.

A Death in the Family was published after Agee's death at age forty-five, and the story of his literary reputation beyond the mid-fifties is largely the work of David McDowell. An understanding of that post-humous reputation is important; this in itself would make an interesting study for a bibliographical scholar, for since his death Agee's works have been appreciated both because of his love of the commonplace and because of his craft as a writer. The establishment of the James Agee Trust to provide funds for Agee's family after his sudden death in 1955, the editing of *A Death in the Family*, the reissue of *Famous Men* in 1960, and the idea for the two volumes of *Agee on Film*, are all projects largely the work of David McDowell. McDowell, who worked in New York publishing since the mid-forties, was a mutual friend of Agee's and Father Flye's. Both Agee and McDowell had been students at St. Andrew's, where they first met in 1936. McDowell recognized the value of *A Death in the Family* and saw its pencil manuscript through the press. The subsequent editing of Robert Fitzgerald of the *Collected Poems* and the *Collected Short Prose*, the *Letters* published by Father Flye, the reissue of *The Morning Watch* and *Permit Me Voyage*, and the many paperback editions of Agee's work, both in the United States and in England, have all added to public knowledge of Agee's writing. All of this attests to significant current interest in Agee's career. How long we might have had to wait if McDowell had not had the foresight to make Agee's writing widely available remains speculation. What we now see is that his skepticism about the use of language resulted in many works which pay special attention to the world and the word.

Agee's career followed few predictable patterns. His writing was hardly the production he dreamt of as a young man, and it is safe to assume that he probably felt his "career" was largely a failure; but it is also clear that there was no failure of integrity or accomplishment. We can wish that he had written more; but we would do well to remember that on many occasions Agee himself insisted that there is no separation between the aesthetic and the moral sense. Perhaps we need to take a closer look at *all* his writing. It is easy to imagine that Agee was used by the Luce publications, but can we honestly maintain such a stance and also maintain that teaching is a more appropriate way for a writer to earn his living? It is true that publishers might have been more daring with Agee's proposals for books, just as the Guggenheim Selection Committee might have been more perceptive when

Agee inundated them with proposals in 1937. But we should remember that Houghton Mifflin did publish *Famous Men* and *The Morning Watch* and that after Agee's death still other work was edited, collected, and recognized.

Above all, we would do well to remind ourselves that Agee would be more than amused at an essay such as this one: definitely his work as journalist had an impact on his writing—but so did places unseen, and literature, and art, and music, and family, and government. As he himself often suggested, all kinds of ways exist through which one can "identify" with others. We are reminded of his placement of Franklin Delano Roosevelt's words at the beginning of the chapter "Money" in *Famous Men:* "I am a farmer myself." Agee found this laughable; but Roosevelt's words also suggest the difficulty inherent in anyone's use of language. Agee wants readers to remember that words such as Roosevelt's will never get at the essence of the particularities of living.

Agee's career developed in large part because of his contact with the Northeast during his years of education and because of his work as journalist and critic. Apparently contact with writers and publishing enterprises made him feel an intensified responsibility to raise questions about the proper use of language. He did so both to honor reality and to criticize a culture which he felt was in too many basic ways superficial, dishonest, and materialistic. His 1944 essay "Pseudo-Folk" is a succinct treatment of many of these ideas. His vision, often a humorous one, is akin to that of Flannery O'Connor. They both learned to look, and by looking carefully to reveal the truth through sharp focus. We remember how many of O'Connor's stories have origins in incidents which can be documented by reading the Milledgeville newspaper. Both Agee and O'Connor had a similar sense of observation and humor. Agee, we remember, proposed doing a parody of an entire issue of a daily newspaper. Why he felt the need for such an exercise is clear; and among his papers at the University of Texas is a newspaper clipping of a photograph of some rather surprised-looking Negroes who are taking part in a ceremony in the Georgia Governor's office, a ceremony occasioned by the fact that their mule had recently died, and the Governor, benevolently, had decided to provide a dollar cash contribution for the relief of these rural poor. Agee clipped that photograph because it is just such a "fact" which makes a good story, but which also stands as an indictment and challenges a writer.

It is safe to say that Agee's years in New York as a professional writer made him increasingly skeptical of the way *all* information is transmitted. All the more reason, however, for his own devotion to language, qualified by doubts about ever getting at "truth." I am reminded of a story of how he once had dinner with a publisher to discuss the possible publication of one of his books. This was probably in 1951, and the book under discussion was *The Morning Watch*. The publisher, we are told, enjoyed his lunch, but reported that he would not consider Agee's new book. Nobody, he said, could talk that successfully and be a good writer too! Maybe better than anything else, this story gets at the mystery of Agee's continual respect for language. Like many southerners, he realized that a story could get at the essence of living better than analysis, or reporting. But he was a professional writer, and he expressed doubts about how to honor actuality. Precisely because of such doubts his best writing suggests the essence of what he respected, actuality itself, but in so doing he warns readers of believing that they have *the* truth.

Scholarship: Agee and, and Agee in

I

James Agee who was always interested in so many aspects of culture and its manifestations in and through the word as well as image might today be mildly surprised at the scholarly interest generated by his diverse writing, yet not to any great degree. Surely, he saw (or heard about) that letter which the enthusiastic W. H. Auden wrote to *The Nation* in 1944 wherein Auden predicted that Agee's movie criticism was so successful that it seemed inevitable that a Ph.D. dissertation would soon follow. Auden was, of course, correct and Agee must have been insightful enough to realize that there was no way to forestall that inevitable dissertation. He knew, as he put it in the preface to *Let Us Now Praise Famous Men*, that the artist who is fully committed to his work runs the very real danger of seeing that work made into a "Modern Library Giant" and then placed on a coffee table.

Agee has fared better than that, yet while we have had a sustained interest in his work for over thirty years, he is still more honored than read, more sanctified, perhaps, than accepted as a significant writer of serious literature. The reasons for this are many, above all I suspect—as indicated in my introduction to this book—that Agee always thought of himself as a "writer" and would not allow himself or his work to be easily classified or labelled. Thus the work remains down to the present a bit of an enigma. When, for example, I was invited to submit possible passages of Agee's work to be included in a proposed anthology of American literature which would, theoretically, bring new pieces into the "canon," I provided poetry, non-fiction, criticism, fiction, and autobiographical writing. All of what I submitted was, in my view, excellent, and all these pieces demonstrated how Agee was throughout his career making significant connections with the rest of American literature and culture. The editors of the projected teaching anthology finally decided to omit Agee all together. Apparently he just didn't fit the new categories which were devised by those editors.

Ten books of Agee's writings are in print, and an eleventh which I have edited, *Selected Literary Documents*, is under contract to be published by the University of Tennessee Press. What is exceedingly interesting about these eleven books is that they are so completely different one from another: poetry; documentary; novella; memory; criticism; fiction; screenplays; letters; prose; verse; as well as journalism. Each of these volumes reflects an important facet of Agee's person. Each makes a different kind of contribution. Each of these different books—from the earliest poetry (sometimes awkward, ambitious, and angry) to the journalism (serviceable and analytical)—says a good bit about James Agee. He could produce a wide variety of work. He was thereby capable of holding the attention of many different kinds of audiences.

The same might be said of the types and varieties of scholarly pieces which have been generated about Agee's writing. There is no need at this point to attempt to analyze this material—approaches which include interest in the literary; textual; filmic; autobiographical; poetic; journalistic, etc. The need is to acknowledge this abundance and perhaps also ask a few questions about Agee's writing which has generated such a wide variety of attention. Bibliographies list this material; Agee's books are still in print; scholars keep reading Agee. The question might be what is at the core of his work which continues to speak to us and to so many?

Part of the answer to the preceding question is that there were so many sides to Agee, and in a sense, he is reflected then in many facets of our own lives. Further, as time passes, new aspects of his accomplishments shine forth.

In the nineteen-fifties when *A Death in the Family* first appeared part of what the reading of that text did was to generate what might be called a reverberation with an earlier era already gone yet nostalgically recreated by Agee's memory and skill as a writer. Preceding that, Agee's *The Morning Watch* stood as an affirmation of religious values precisely at a moment in the collective American consciousness when the religious seemed to be needed.

Agee's *Let Us Now Praise Famous Men* also struck chords in the American consciousness of the sixties. Republished in 1960, it became a kind of "Bible" about the dispossessed during an era of affluence. Agee, as an almost cult figure, was perceived during this era (probably incorrectly) as a rebel squashed by the vagaries of American taste and big publishing. Little of this has much basis in Truth, yet the truth to be observed is that there is so much in Agee's writing that his readers—the general public, the teachers, the students—always seem to find something of great value with each additional encounter or rereading.

II

As indicated earlier the amount of writing generated about Agee has been considerable. He is, therefore, recognized as a significant "minor" writer, yet apparently he can never be easily classified, and much remains to be done in terms of reading his work precisely because he wrote in so many different ways and because the work has been regarded so differently decade by decade.

The amount of writing about Agee over the years has been significant, but it has not been an extraordinary amount. As a noteworthy minor writer Agee has generated some 40 doctoral dissertations and approximately 10 monographs, much less, for example, than his contemporaries Richard Wright or Nathanael West, or later Flannery O'Connor, someone with whom he might be compared because of region and theme. Yet vastly more interest has been expressed concerning Agee than for that of many of his immediate contemporaries. This fact is extremely interesting.

When the novel made from unfinished manuscripts, *A Death in the Family*, was published in 1957, except for those in New York close to him, Agee was virtually unknown. When *A Death in the Family* appeared it was, perhaps, the detailed analysis that Dwight Macdonald (who had known him since the mid-nineteen-thirties) and the commentary of critics like W. M. Frohock (who had been one of his classmates at Harvard) which brought the book to the public's attention. Agee was perceived by these, his earliest commentators, as the victim of forces (in American culture, in writing, in publishing) which he could not control, yet the beauty of *A Death in the Family* was that there was something in that text which spoke to a generation which had begun to sense its own loss of roots and religion and which yearned for a sense of region. Such readers realized that they had need of an awareness of tradition and community.

Through words, Agee found ways to honor the ordinary. He found ways to catch the beauty of moments which others perhaps had ignored. Slowly as more of his writing has been made available, he, as a person lost and lamented, has become less significant, while the diversity of his writing and commentary has become more appreciated. The range of his accomplishments is finally what is most interesting.

All my own writing about Agee, some now collected in this book, has been done because I admire the art and beauty of his perception and performances and the poetry of his expression. My first systematic writing about Agee was on *Let Us Now Praise Famous Men* in 1962-1963. My doctoral work was a project devoted to sorting, reading, editing, and then analyzing a mass of unpublished Agee manuscripts (1965-1966). In context I see everything he wrote as having value.

Out of context many problems emerge: it may be just as well, therefore, to avoid forcing Agee into this or that category. The recent Laurence Bergreen biography is an excellent example of too much attention placed on flaws in his life and not enough concern with the beauty and permanence of the writing. In the many reviews which I have done over the years of books by and about Agee, my concern has been to see how new work, by him or by scholars about him, reveals important aspects of the relationship of work and life; yet I've never been interested in the lurid or sensational. Whether or not Agee really was ever hanging from the window of the *Fortune* offices in the Chrysler building one day in the middle nineteen-thirties (in despair we are led to imagine for reasons not given!) is, in my view, much less important than the very real fact that, as Robert Fitzgerald put it, he would have written a book like *Let Us Now Praise Famous Men* even if he had never had the chance to go to Alabama.

The considerable work of David McDowell which led to the publication of *A Death in the Family* and the reprinting of *Let Us Now Praise Famous Men*, as well as the gathering of the two volumes entitled *Agee on Film*, as well as the editorial work of Robert Fitzgerald which made *The Collected Short Prose* and *The Collected Poems* volumes available, must be recognized as *the* most important contributions to making Agee accessible. Likewise, the effort of Father James Harold Flye, who edited the *Letters of James Agee to Father Flye*, in 1962 is of inestimable value. All of this has led to many other projects and has helped to sustain interest in Agee. Subsequent scholarly work by Alfred Barson, Genevieve Moreau, Mark A. Doty and others has demonstrated the importance of Agee's diverse kinds of writing, yet it remains correct to say that we still do not have an adequate overview of Agee's accomplishment.

In some ways the recent biography by Bergreen is more a distraction because of the extravagances in Agee's life than a help in relation to the writing. I do not think we are ever to take seriously the misguided claims of Bergreen who reads passages from *Let Us Now Praise Famous Men* and *A Death in the Family* as if they were biographical fact. Besides, we know from much recent scholarship about autobiography that it is the fictional which feeds any true autobiographical impulse.

III

Agee's work, as I have insisted, will not be easily classified. The fact that now he is generating interdisciplinary studies by scholars such as Gordon Taylor and J. D. Ward reminds us of his complex interests and of his value to so many different types of readers. Much more will be done. A book is in process on the subject of *Agee and the South*, to be published by the University of Tennessee Press. Here aspects of his Southern roots will be examined.[1]

Much more remains to be done. Agee's writings need to be studied in relation to religion, region, and other writers, his contemporaries, as well as classic writers. I myself am writing about *Let Us Now Praise Famous Men* and Agee's consciousness of technique. I also see the need for a critical edition of *A Death in the Family* which would add materials to this problematic text. This will necessitate, perhaps, a new version of that text which would relegate the present "Preface" entitled "Knoxville: Summer, 1915" to the position of an appendix. Such a critical edition of *A Death in the Family* would have to retain the basic text as we know it, but as some of the articles in this book made clear, that text needs to be corrected. Further, much more material could be added to the memory or "italicized" sections.

We also need to see some of Agee's correspondence published in an accurate edition. The letters to Walker Evans, Robert Fitzgerald, and Dwight Macdonald alone would make an excellent volume. If such letters were made available, study of them in conjunction with more careful interviewing of those who knew Agee, might result in a much fuller biographical picture.

More can also be done with Agee's movie work, criticism and scenarios. Detailed study of the unpublished materials for his Stephen Crane screenplays; *The Quiet One*; the unproduced *Noa, Noa,* and the *Lincoln Omnibus* television work would each help us to understand the total body of Agee's writing (and him as well).

What does all this mean? We are at an interesting moment in Agee scholarship. We are definitely in need of more careful studies of the individual works; we need more textual information about *A Death in the Family* and the other major prose works. As J. Hillis Miller said of the work of William Carlos Williams, finally to understand Williams we have to read *all* of it.

If James Agee's unpublished writings had been made more readily available a more complex picture of Agee's achievement would now exist. If, for example, David McDowell had encouraged a critical edition of *A Death in the Family* to be completed, or if the present trustee of the Agee trust were more open to use of Agee's early and unfinished writings, his reputation as well as interest in his life and his place in American letters might be more secure. Other trustees for other writers have been more foresightful, as, for example, has been the case with the legacy of Thomas Merton or Ernest Hemingway. Agee is thus still in need of much careful reading, editing, and analysis.

I hope this volume of essays assists in that exercise, and I hope it leads to still other projects which will help more readers to come to know Agee.

Note

[1] The essay, printed in this book at pages 136-148, is being revised and expanded for the forthcoming University of Tennessee Press book.

Index